THE
TWELVE
ENLIGHTENMENTS
for
HEALING SOCIETY

Also by the Author

*Brain Respiration: A Powerful
Technique to Energize Your Brain*

Dahn Meditation and Exercise

Healing Society

THE
TWELVE
ENLIGHTENMENTS

for

HEALING SOCIETY

Dr. ILCHI LEE

Creator and Grand Master of
Dahn Hak and Brain Respiration

WALSCH
BOOKS

an imprint of
HAMPTON ROADS
PUBLISHING COMPANY, INC.
www.hrpub.com

Cover design by Marjoram Productions
Cover art by Marjoram Productions

Hampton Roads Publishing Company, Inc.
1125 Stoney Ridge Road
Charlottesville, VA 22902

434-296-2772
fax: 434-296-5096
e-mail: hrpc@hrpub.com
www.hrpub.com

If you are unable to order this book from your local
bookseller, you may order directly from the publisher.
Call 1-800-766-8009, toll-free.

Library of Congress Catalog Card Number: 2002100964

ISBN 1-57174-335-9

10 9 8 7 6 5 4 3 2 1

Printed on acid-free paper in the United States

THE
TWELVE
ENLIGHTENMENTS
for
HEALING SOCIETY

Table of Contents

Humanity Conference
and a Declaration of Humanity

World-renowned scholars, thinkers, and social activists were brought together in Seoul, Korea on June 15, 2001 to attend the First Annual New Millennium World Peace Humanity Conference, exploring the concrete influence that spirituality can have in our current political, economic, and cultural makeup. New Millennium Peace Foundation (NMPF), a nongovernmental, independent organization founded by Dr. Ilchi Lee and Neale Donald Walsch in 1997, invited prestigious academics, journalists, activists, and experts in the fields of religion, journalism, culture, environment, and, most importantly, human capacities to make presentations and engage in discussions with the participants.

Distinguished guests included, among others, Dr. Ilchi Lee, president of the NMPF and co-host of the conference; Neale Donald Walsch, the best-selling author of the *Conversations with God* series, founder of ReCreation, and co-host; Maurice Strong, a senior advisor to the Secretary General of the United Nations and the president of UN University for Peace; Seymour Topping, administrator of the Pulitzer Prizes and professor of international journalism at Columbia University Graduate School of Journalism; Reverend Wyatt Tee Walker, senior pastor of Canaan Baptist

Church, noted civil rights activist, and former executive secretary to Martin Luther King; Jean Houston, the world's leading researcher in human potential and co-director of the Foundation for Mind Research; Hanne Strong, president of Manitou Foundation and an environmental activist; and Audrey Ronning Topping, a Pulitzer Prize-winning photojournalist and author. Attending as a special guest was former U.S. Vice President Al Gore, who was recently a visiting professor at Columbia University Graduate School of Journalism.

The main outcome of the conference was the adoption of the Declaration of Humanity, a brief document that can be described as the Magna Carta for Earth and Earth-Humans, those whose highest common self-identification is that they have surpassed the artificial boundaries of nationhood, religion, and ethnicity and see themselves as citizens of the Earth. This document was officially adopted by the special guests, conference participants, and over 12,000 enthusiastic Earth-Humans with much fanfare and joy. So far, more than 100,000 people have signed on. Here is the full text of the Declaration of Humanity:

Declaration of Humanity
June 15, 2001

1. I declare that I am a spiritual being, an essential and eternal part of the Soul of Humanity, one and indivisible.

2. I declare that I am a human being, whose rights and security ultimately depend on assuring the human rights of all people of Earth.

3. I declare that I am a child of the Earth, with the will and awareness to work for goals that benefit the entire community of Earth on Earth.

4. I declare that I am a healer, with the power and purpose to heal the many forms of divisions and conflicts that exist on Earth.

5. I declare that I am a protector, with the knowledge and responsibility to help Earth recover her natural harmony and beauty.

6. I declare that I am an activist in service to the world, with the commitment and the ability to make a positive difference in my society.

If you would like to sign your name as a sign of support and agreement, please visit the website, www.healingsociety.org.

Preface

As I write this, the year 2001 is coming to an end. History will record this year as the year in which the World Trade Center towers fell. History will know this year as the Year of September 11. History will be a witness to the massive grief and shock that we all felt when we first heard the news with incredulity and foreboding. History will surely judge us by our actions in response to these brutal acts.

In this hour of continuing personal grief for so many, I join with the rest of America in praying for the souls of the departed and their families, and for the quick recovery of the injured. As someone who spends the majority of his time in the US and feels love for the often-breathtaking beauty of the land and the everlasting warmth of her people, I was personally shaken by such a tragedy. This is indeed a time of grief and reflection not only for a nation, but for all of humanity.

On the day of the attacks, the then-mayor of New York said the final body count would be more than we could bear. I had not heard such foreboding words in many years, and they were all the more tragic because it was the probable truth behind his words that brought such a sense of heavy expectancy. The attacks were horrifying to us not because of the magnitude of destruction they wrought, not because they occurred in our backyard, not because they threatened our sense of security in our very homes, but ultimately because of our inability to understand the depth of hatred that lay behind these actions. There is a wall of unknowability of the sheer rage exhibited by such actions. What could drive someone, a human being, to purposely sacrifice his own life to kill and maim tens of thousands of innocent others in order to make a point?

When I see the horrific aftermath of this and other attacks, I often ask, "What point could possibly have been so important to cause such bloodshed?" What cause could possibly have been so crucial to cause bodies and limbs to rain down on the streets of New York City? What national or international interest is so paramount that innocent babies have to be riddled with nails from a crude bomb or a child be shot and bleed to death next to his father?

We feel anger, rage, and a need to revenge ourselves upon the perpetrators of these terrible deeds. We want justice done, which often means inflicting the same or greater amount of pain upon the parties we believe responsible. However, when the emotions of the moment pass—and they will pass—and we have performed these "acts of justice," we are often left with an empty feeling of loss and sadness. Ultimately we are left asking, "Why do such things happen, and continue to happen?"

These things continue to happen because some basic needs of a large number of our fellow human beings are not being met. We all have basic needs that have to be fulfilled, chief among them are the needs for safety and recognition. When someone threatens our safety, we respond with anger. When we are helpless against such threats, we feel despair or fear. We then ask someone to recognize our fear and come to our aid. If no one does, we feel a betrayal. A combination of despair, fear, and betrayal will cause someone to lash out against real and imagined enemies, causing more of the same in others. It is a vicious cycle indeed. A cycle of hatred unleashed can wreak destruction for generations to come. Just witness the world today.

A choice lies before us today. Should we add to the cycle by blaming someone and taking our vengeance? I am not asking the USA to not defend herself and her citizens from such attacks. I am not asking the USA to not respond appropriately to those responsible for such deeds. However, I am asking the USA to recognize the fear, desperation, and betrayal in large parts of the world that precipitated today's tragedy. The only way to dissolve such intense negativity will be to give each human being on Earth a sense of security and recognition—security to feel safe in her own little corner of Earth and a general recognition of each human being as a unique person.

I am asking the USA as the only superpower in the world to take the lead in stopping this wheel of vendetta, once and for all, through acts of wisdom and understanding. More blood need not be shed. May God's blessings fall upon the victims of today's horrible tragedy. May God's strength be with those who have to deal with the aftermath. And may God's mercy guide the hands of those who seek to bring those responsible to answer for their deeds.

For now, let us pray that we, as humanity, find the wisdom and courage in our belief in our Oneness to co-create a world where such tragedies are unknown. Let us realize that we are all Earth-Humans—of Earth and not of any one nation, religion, or ethnicity.

Let us pray.

Ilchi Lee
Sedona, Arizona
December 2001

A New Trend in Spirituality—From Meditation to Healing

Someone asked me in a recent lecture, his face hard set with doubt, "Are you really enlightened?" I answered him with a question: "Do you know what enlightenment is?" He said no. Then I told him, "If you don't know what enlightenment is, you would not believe me if I were to tell you that I am enlightened or believe me if I told you that I was not enlightened." He pressed on, again with an expression of someone reluctantly mining for the truth: "Then what was it that you were enlightened to?" Laughing, I answered him, "I was enlightened to the fact that there is nothing to be enlightened about."

Although the reluctant truth-seeker did not continue with his interrogation, I sensed that many in the audience had the same question or curiosity in mind about the nature of enlightenment. I pointed to the ceiling with my index finger and asked, "How many fingers do you see?" The audience giggled, some looking mildly offended and others looking childishly eager to find the deep, Zen koan answer behind such a simple question. "I see only one," I continued. "How about you? When there are no special conditions or devices preventing us from seeing something as it is, there is no difference in what you see and what I see. Truth is thus. Unless you

THE TWELVE ENLIGHTENMENTS FOR HEALING SOCIETY

have an impediment or a handicap with your sight, without any preconceived prejudice to see more than one finger, one finger will look like one finger to you all. This is enlightenment."

Enlightenment Is Choice

To see something, you don't have to know the particulars of how your eyes work. In fact, the foremost ophthalmologists, biologists, and bioengineers do not agree on a single explanation as to how human beings see. However, we can see without knowing how we see. We know that we can see and that we are now looking at a single finger pointing towards the ceiling. Do not imagine that the world seen by an enlightened being is in any way different from a world seen by you. A finger is just a finger, no matter whose eyes focus upon it. Enlightenment is no different from the process of seeing, hearing, and feeling. To be in the natural state of seeing, hearing, and feeling—this in itself is enlightenment.

Therefore, enlightenment does not take an effort. If you seek enlightenment through some type of effort, then it is not true enlightenment. An effort is needed to make something incomplete complete, something imperfect perfect. However, enlightenment is already perfect and complete, not needing any efforts at improvement. The reason that we cannot see a single finger as a finger is not because of the lack of "enlightenment," but because of prejudices, egos, and attachments. If you can divest your consciousness of these obstacles, you will realize your consciousness by itself is complete and perfect, the realization of which is enlightenment. Therefore, enlightenment is not something that you have to strive for; it is something felt and realized naturally without any effort. This is why your enlightenment and my enlightenment, your truth and my truth, are not different. Because truth is unchanging, it can be communicated and transmitted to others and expressed in actions. If enlightenment cannot be communicated and truth cannot be shared among all, then such things are merely personal illusions of grandeur.

Enlightenment is seeing, hearing, and feeling—a natural state of being, a realization at which we can arrive by allowing ourselves to acknowledge it. That's why I say that enlightenment is a choice—the choice to acknowledge or deny the enlightenment that we already possess within. Therefore, enlightenment is not a finish line but a starting point.

When you acknowledge the perfect and complete enlightenment within you and realize that you are the master of your own choices and life, then you are ready to embark on a life of spiritual and universal responsibility. The important thing is not whether you consciously realize that you have joined the elite ranks of the "enlightened ones," but to make your daily choices based upon what you see, hear, and feel, and to take responsibility for your choices.

Enlightenment Is Not Important—
Your Character Is!

We make judgments and choices based upon what we see, hear, and feel. Life in itself can be called a series of continuing choices. Whether we realize our own innate enlightenment or not, we continue to see, hear, and feel, and base our judgments and make our choices upon these underpinnings. Unless you have a handicap or a deficiency in your senses, there is no difference in what you see, hear, and feel and what I see, hear, and feel, regardless of whether you realize that you are enlightened or not.

In other words, enlightenment does not by itself guarantee you will make the best choices. Of course, the ability to see, hear, or feel something as it is will aid you in making a wise decision; however, it does not necessarily lead you to make the best possible choice. Ultimately, the process of making a choice depends not upon an acknowledgment or a realization, but upon your sense of discipline and character. Your choice is based upon your character.

The root of your character is your habits. A once-in-a-blue-moon choice does not reveal your character. Numerous choices will gel into a habit, out of which the flower of your character will bloom. A good character is a fruit borne from the tree of good habits. Your goal should not be to attain enlightenment, for enlightenment is something given to you already—whether you realize it or not, admit it or not. Enlightenment exists within you, independent of your choice; it is already a flower in the divine Garden of God. Your responsibility lies in nurturing a good character, bearing the best possible fruit or the most beautiful flower from the perfect seed in the Garden of God.

Your soul is this divine seed. We call this divinity. All souls are perfect. Depending into which soil you plant this seed and what care you give it, it will bear fruits or flowers of different sizes, shapes, smells, and tastes. The process of planting and nurturing this seed is a series of endless choices. An accumulation of such choices will become your habits, the root of the tree from which the flower, your character, will blossom.

From the Pursuit of Enlightenment to Actualization of Enlightenment—From Meditation to Healing

To be able to nurture the blossoming of a beautiful flower from the perfect seed of the soul is an exquisite accomplishment. However, something nobler awaits those with the desire to see, hear, and feel further. That is to become a gardener in the Garden of God and to help other seeds to achieve their perfect beauty. This is the true meaning of Healing.

The meaning of healing lies in helping others discover the divinity within and apply it to their everyday lives. If we call the realization of the divinity within "Enlightenment," then we can call the actualization of this enlightenment, "Healing."

Until now, we have been obsessed with attaining enlightenment; however, there is no true purpose in realizing that one finger is one finger unless you now put that one finger to good use. Action is the key. If enlightenment is a choice, then your actions will reveal your enlightenment. How else are you going to prove your own enlightenment other than through your actions? You can't prove it through words or scientific evidence. What else is there except action with which you can prove your enlightenment? This is why the time has now come for us to concentrate more on healing than emphasizing the pursuit of enlightenment.

We need a new trend in spirituality, from the pursuit of enlightenment to actualization of enlightenment, from meditation to healing. When meditation was a fad, it was very difficult to distinguish between genuine and fake, real and fraud, for meditation is an experience that is intensely personal and non-transferable and not subject to scientific inquiry. We no longer have time for such flighty enjoyment. We no longer have time to discuss the truth as an exercise in wordsmithing. We no longer have the luxury to listen to the sounds of our own voices as we debate the meaning of the truth in catchy, seemingly profound terms, ultimately going nowhere concrete.

If truth is something that we can readily see, hear, and feel in our natural state, then what else is there left to say? What other explanations do you need to explain the phenomenon of seeing one finger as one finger? Unless you purposely try to see differently or distort your sight, you will see only one finger.

So, let us take this "one-finger" sight and gaze at our collective home, Earth. I see problems. How about you? With this sight, what do you see of our society, our world, our Earth?

Many "enlightened" people try to avoid taking responsibility for the problems that we face today by spouting the concept I summarize as "Existence is by definition perfect." Which means that we cannot destroy the ultimate harmony of existence no matter what, for cosmic law ultimately will balance everything out in perfect cause and effect and give and take. This is "truth," yet it is irrelevant to the situation we face today. I have no interest in such abstract discussions. Perhaps people who support this view haven't considered that we all have roles to play in making the "perfect" in the perfectness of existence. If we have a cancerous cell in our bodies, the perfectness of our immune systems can be evidenced by the destruction of that cell; however, a higher perfectness of our

5

healing power can also be demonstrated by converting the cancerous cell into a healthy one. In both cases, the cancer cell will be gone and harmony restored.

If humanity, in its wanton destruction of the environment, can be considered a cancer in the body of Earth, then it would only be divine justice and an expression of the perfectness of existence that human beings become extinct, through our own making or by divine retribution. This would set the cosmic balance right. However, we can also right the skewed balance by achieving a collective conscious evolution and working together to help our society and Earth recover their lost health. The final reading on the cosmic balance will be the same, but which would you choose?

No one way is "truer" than another, but which way would you choose to express the truth? If death is the truth and life is also the truth, which would you choose? In which form do you want the truth to express itself to you? Although truth is eternal and unchanging, its expression is constantly shifting. Independent of our choices, truth always finds a way to express its perfectness, no matter where it is recognized. It is always pouring in wherever there is a lack, and pouring out where there is an excess.

In places of overflow, pouring out will be an expression of the truth of the cosmic balance, and in places of dearth, pouring in will be an expression of the truth. If we see a problem in ourselves, our society, and our Earth, then truth is solving these problems. Healing is expression of the truth. When more of us open our eyes to the truth in healing and seek to join others who have this sense for truth, then healing will not be relegated to the scrap heap of history as another fad, but will give birth to a worldwide cultural phenomenon that will heal ourselves, our society, and our Earth.

Healing has many dimensions and associated methods. Just as soil, sunlight, and moisture act in concert to nurture a seed into a beautiful flower, we can use light, sound, and vibration in any combination to heal the body and soul. We can also use soothing music, inspiring messages, and various activities to heal. We have healing on an individual basis and healing on a societal or global plane. Healing society or the world is like working as a gardener to help flowers bloom and trees to bear fruit by making the environment for growth into the best one possible. Under unfavorable conditions, even a healthy seed will not be able to mature into its full potential. Only when the right combination of soil, sunlight, and moisture exists will the seed express its full potential.

This is why we need like-minded individuals to join together to form an enlightened community, for the community that we live in and the people whom we communicate with on an everyday basis shape the conditions and the environment under which the flower of character will have to grow. In a fundamental sense, Earth and the community of human beings comprise the most basic environment in which we, as humanity, share as we try to nurture the seed of the soul. Therefore, healing, in its most fundamental and largest sense, is a healing of Earth and humanity. If the whole world is in winter, no matter how hard you try to maintain warmth inside your home, how long can you escape the cold? Even if a rose miraculously blossoms in a field of snow, how long do you think it can maintain its beauty?

We seek not only to help individuals reach their divine potential, but to cultivate the best environment possible for all of humanity to reach its collective divine potential before this garden called Earth becomes too barren for any life to exist and too desolate for any seed of divine potential to blossom forth. Let us move quickly, but with a purpose, with a sense of urgency, but without fear, for we already work in God's Garden and have all the tools that we need.

Do you believe in your divinity? Do you want a confirmation? Then, let your healing efforts for Earth and humanity be your evidence for the existence of the Creator within.

Start of a Creative Life—Freedom from the Need to Learn

We think that we need to learn in order to lead fulfilling lives. Modern urban life asks of us many hours of "learning." We have to learn how to use the computer, ride the subway, use the ATM machine, how to sing and dance—we can't even sing or dance without having someone teach us how! However, those things that maintain life itself are not ever forgotten because we have never learned them in the first place.

Life's most basic functions, such as the beating of the heart, maintaining the blood pressure and body temperature, and regulations of the hormonal levels, are not things that we have to learn how to do. Eating, breathing, and drinking are never learned. Because they are never learned, they are never forgotten. You can consciously choose to breathe quickly or slowly; eat more, less, or none; and drink two, four, or eight cups of water a day. We can fool ourselves into thinking that we do a lot to maintain our own lives. However, the most important things in life are done automatically for us. Have you ever observed your body breathing by itself, without any effort on your part? Can you sense the incredible mystery and beauty of a breath? Think for a moment . . . think about life itself. Who does this life belong to? Who allows us the simple beauty of the breath?

Learning Chains that Bind Us

I always throw some "play" of sorts into my lectures. It doesn't require any special tools or instruments. It only requires that we use our bodies as playthings: bang on the stomach as you would on a drum; stretch out your cheeks like rubber bands; knead your body like dough or caress it gently as you would a flower. If I do use something, it is a crude, ingenious Vietnamese wooden xylophone called a *tapo*, or a wooden flute. There is no set melody or rhythm. No set notes or songs. I just play it to the natural rhythm of my inner being. After a while, it coalesces into music, song, even a dance.

I once told an audience, "Now I will give you five minutes of free time during which you can exercise or move your body freely." There was a bewildered silence, with people standing and looking at each other with blank faces as if they had never exercised or moved their bodies before. How peculiar. They were confounded by the simple request to move their bodies as they willed. How would you have reacted? Think. Imagine that you have just received such a request. Get up and try it. How would you start? It might stump you for a moment. Should you rotate your shoulders clockwise three times before circling your waist with your hands? Should you start with your wrists and work you way up to your shoulders? Should you boogie?

We are too used to learning and being taught. We feel nervous, or sometimes even guilty, when we don't do things exactly the way we were taught. It is such over-reliance on the need to learn that is making our society into a world of experts, evermore selective, divisive, and complicated. If we go on this way, maybe there will come a day when we will all have to learn how to breathe. In fact, that is what I do—teach people to breathe. However, I don't teach people complicated techniques for breathing, but allow them to feel the natural rhythm of their breath, lightly and deeply. That is all.

If you allow your consciousness to drift toward your lower abdomen during breathing, then your breath will naturally delve deeper within you. If you allow your consciousness to experience

9

the gratitude and joy of breathing, then your breath will naturally become light. Your breathing will naturally achieve a deep lightness if you inhale as an expression of thanks to your body and exhale as an expression of thanks to the Heavens above. Then you can lose yourself in your breath. You can follow your breath into and out of your body, losing yourself until you become the breath itself.

Learning Does Not Necessarily Help Us Choose Wisely

To lead a life of creativity, you first have to free yourself from the need to learn. When you had to make an important choice in your life, what made you pause and feel afraid? More often than not, it was probably the idea that you didn't "know" enough. However, just as we don't need to learn to manipulate the biological functions needed to maintain life, we don't need to be filled with expert knowledge to make the most important decisions in our lives.

Granted, the world we live in today is filled with myriad choices that require you to have a great amount of knowledge. Take a fund manager, for example. If you don't know what a fund manager is, you can't say to yourself that you want to be one. However, the important thing is not to confuse your goal with the means. Say you want to become a fund manager; can this ambition truly be your goal and the reason for your existence? In many cases, we are mistaken into thinking that the means we use is the goal itself; we eventually realize the mistake after many fruitless years of trying to fill a certain emptiness in our hearts that won't go away no matter how "successful" we have become.

This is what I mean when I say that you don't need expert knowledge to choose your purpose in life. Expert, specific knowledge is necessary when you have already chosen your goal and are looking for the best method to achieve it. It is not necessary for you to choose your life's goal. When someone asks you what your goal in life is, what would you reply? That you don't know yet? That you don't have enough information to decide? That you need more data to compute? That you need to learn more?

But we already know that learning does not necessarily make it easier to make the most important choices in your life. Do we need that much knowledge to live "right?" Learning can be an excuse for putting off your choice. No matter how much relevant information you have learned or how much knowledge you have attained, you will always feel a conflict and a modicum of self-doubt at the moment of making a choice. Ultimately, it isn't your knowledge that makes the choice; it is your will and character.

The moment when we truly become masters of our lives and lead creative and "masterful" lives is when we free ourselves from the compulsive need to learn. When you stop thinking that you need to learn something, that you don't know something, you will allow the inner light of divine wisdom within you to shine forth brightly, out of which your power of creation will bloom. I have never learned how to play the *tapo* or the flute. Since I never learned how to play these instruments, I never knew or cared whether I played them correctly or not. The same goes for my audience. Since they have no idea whether I am playing correctly or not, they enjoy listening to the music and rhythms that I enjoy creating. We all get to enjoy the spontaneous joy of creation.

The Limits of Our High-Tech, High-Energy World

The loss of our natural creativity and our over-reliance on experts and their complicated, elaborate knowledge have made our lives parasitic, wasteful, and feeble. Think how much information, skill, and energy we need to satisfy our most basic life functions such as obtaining food, eating food, disposing of remaining food, and getting rid of bodily wastes. We probably use ten thousand times more energy than other mammals on the planet to take care of our basic needs, making our lives feeble and weak.

For example, can you maintain your life if all electricity and gas to your home were to be permanently cut off right now? In modern life, electricity and gas are not used only for lighting; they are intimately connected to how we eat and drink. If we don't have gasoline, we can't drive to the supermarket. Even if we were to somehow make our way to the supermarket, the shelves would be empty of foodstuffs because there would be no way to get the merchandise there. We wouldn't be able to cook even if we had all the ingredients. Since the water company would be without electricity, they would not be able to deliver water to our homes, depriving us of washing and drinking water. How long do you think you could last under such conditions?

Those prepared or fortunate might last a while on stored foodstuffs and drinks, but what happens when these run out? Eventually, you might have to venture out into nature to look for things to eat. But even if you made it to a forest, would you know which plants are edible and which are poisonous? How would you shelter yourself from the cold? How would you light a fire? How would you take care of a wound?

Our system of living must inevitably change. Our current system of "civilized" living, wasteful and destructive, cannot be maintained at its most basic level. Nevertheless, what we call "civilization" is ceaselessly expanding itself and co-opting more and more of the Earth. To maintain itself, it is using evermore energy and material, making us sink ever deeper into its system. It is obvious that Earth cannot support this for much longer.

The situation is analogous to a nuclear reactor whose core has melted and is in danger of exploding. However, no matter how urgent the situation has become, we cannot change our whole system of living overnight. This would be like attempting to arrest the core meltdown by throwing cold water on it. It wouldn't work, and it could bring about a disaster. Change is obviously needed, but this calls for a carefully thought-out plan of implementation first. However, what we need most of all is to make the choice to want to change. This choice is not something that we can leave to experts because we don't "know" enough. It has to be our choice.

If we don't make a choice now, sooner or later, worsening conditions might force us to adapt to a new system of living, which will necessarily be far worse and difficult to adapt to because we would not be ready or prepared for such a change. This is why it is necessary for us to make the choice to want to change. Now.

First Things First: Let's Change Our Character, Habits, and Technology

What is required for us to become friendly with Earth again and to maintain the existence of the human race? In order for our lives on Earth to once again gain stability and harmony, we need to effect a fundamental change in three things: our character, habits, and technology.

Our character controls the type and strength of our greed and ambitions; our habits form the root of our character; and our technology was created to realize our ambitions. These must all change. I place these three factors in this order—character, habit, and technology—not to denote some kind of chronological order for change, but to list them by fundamentality. The reason that many attempts to change this world have run out of steam is that they sought to reform superficial technological aspects instead of attacking the underlying, fundamental factors such as human character and habits.

We thought we could save the world through technological advances. This approach is analogous to changing the type of fuel while leaving the type of engine untouched. It is the same as leaving our current destructive way of life unchallenged while looking for ways to prolong it through technology. Of course, technology is helpful and needed. However, what is most important is the goal— what do we seek to achieve in life, and what is the purpose of life? We might need expert knowledge in dealing with technological changes, but we don't need such knowledge in deciding our life's purpose; only your choice is required. Technological advances will only help us if their introduction is superseded by a fundamental

13

change in our character and habits. Only then can we comfortably and constructively utilize the technology available to us.

First, a fundamental change in your character comes about through a process of choice known as enlightenment. Through this choice, you decide who you are and how you want to live your life. You choose what your purpose in life is. You realize that you are the only one who is qualified and an authority to answer these questions about yourself. Your choice is your answer. When you choose enlightenment, you will start a fundamental shift in your character.

Second, a change in your habits will come about gradually as you start practicing your choice to be enlightened in your everyday life. The "enlightened" you that you have chosen to be is probably far different from who you are right now. Therefore, you need practice and changes in your habits to become that "enlightened" person you decided was you. Habit re-formation is the first step to actualizing your choice of enlightenment. Only through constant vigil, discipline, and practice will you effect this change in your habits. After a while, your habits will have changed, and these new habits will in turn help your character to reform, creating a cycle of constructive re-formation.

Third, changes in technology start with the rediscovery of soft technologies. Changes in technology must start with something that is simple, comfortable, and that brings about an immediate and visible impact on our lives. Currently, there are many innovative low-energy technologies on the market that are underutilized. If we combine our knowledge and skills, I am sure that we can invent even more ingenious low-energy alternatives.

Yet we don't necessarily have to look outside us to find a change in technology that could have an immediate impact. We don't have to rely on the latest technology and experts to invent a newer and more advanced "machine." Let's take a look at health, for example. By using simple skills and "human" technology, we can vastly improve our health, thereby reducing the enormous amount of money used to keep us healthy every year.

Through simple movements such as self-patting, calisthenics, and breathing exercises, we can rejuvenate our natural healing powers, which, in turn, will help us maintain good health throughout our lives. This is nothing new. It has been scientifically proven and anecdotally demonstrated, repeatedly. Such methods cost nothing and do not require painful surgery or medication. Nor are they psychologically burdensome. They don't even require tools or instruments. All you need is a little practice to make them into habits. If such simple things can save you time and energy, allow you to live a more confident and creative life, and save society a lot of money, isn't this a great thing?

If a change in our lives requires individually or socially painful sacrifices, it will be very difficult to effect it no matter how necessary that change might be. However, if we start on the road of change with simple, enjoyable, and preliminary changes with visible results, we will soon be prepared to tackle larger, more fundamental changes. This is the reason that I declare that "change" must start with health-related "soft technologies"; this is why I teach correct breathing "technology."

Everything Starts with Freedom from the Need to Learn

The start of any change begins with the freedom from the need to learn. You have to start with something that is easy, enjoyable, and natural, like breathing. After you experience and internalize the effects brought about by these new changes, you will sense something larger in your life and the need to share it with others. As you embark on this road, your attitude toward life will change, your worldview will change, and you will have become a pebble tossed into the world pond that causes a new "enlightened" cultural ripple to spread outward.

As you let go of your dependence on "learning" and choose to change your character, habits, and technologies, you will often face doubt and hesitation. However, your instinctive trust in the energy of your own life force, especially confirmed by your conscious experiences, will help you overcome these doubts and hesitations. When we feel the strong, pulsating energy of life and marvel at the process of life that does not require our conscious manipulation, we have no choice but to trust it and be humbled by it.

Trust in life and listen to it. Listen to the rhythm of life. Listen to your own breath and pulse. Learn to resonate consciously with that rhythm . . . no, don't learn. Stop learning and just listen and observe. Observe how you breathe, how your heart beats, how your skin tingles. Now, express your life's rhythm freely, for it is in that freedom that truth resides, life lives, and creation is consummated. When enough of us choose to live this way, our society and our Earth will regain its life force and start on the road to healing.

A New Definition of Life—
From the Heart to the Brain

This may be an offbeat question, but if we were to classify and weigh every chemical compound that makes up the human body, how much would they fetch at the drugstore? The body is about 70 percent water, proteins, small amounts of calcium and other trace minerals—all commonplace and inexpensive. If we separate these chemical compounds into separate bowls, weigh them, and sell them, how much would the going price be? By most estimates, it is less than a dollar. It shouldn't be too expensive.

It might be macabre to put a price on the human body in such a fashion, for we know that we are far more than the sum of our parts. No one in his right mind would call the separate bowls of chemical compounds that make up the body a human being. We further know that we cannot just mix these chemicals together and expect to see a human being emerge, just as a haphazard combination of concrete, steel, and wood will not automatically coalesce into a fully formed house. So, the question arises: what else do we need to create a human body?

Three Factors to the Human Body: Ingredients, Information, and Energy

Just as we need a blueprint to build a house properly, we need a map and instructions to build a human body. The device that contains this information is called DNA. DNA is an information storage device, much like a disk containing computer software. But we have to understand that DNA is a device that stores genetic information; it is not the information itself. Although we can touch the disk that holds the software, we cannot touch the software. The same thing goes for your genetic information. You cannot touch the information itself.

Now you have two things needed to make up your body: material ingredients and information. Let's go forward, then, and see if we can make a human body out of these two things. On one side is the ingredients and on the other, the information. They could sit next to each other for the next million years but nothing will happen without an impetus of some kind. You can have tons of building materials and a blueprint, but nothing will happen without constructive effort of some kind. You can put a disk into a computer, but you can't get the information in it to execute anything without energy to connect the hardware with the software. Only when energy is added can you bring the contained information to the fore.

Energy is, therefore, the bridge by which information comes into action using the ingredients at hand. The same goes for our bodies. Energy is needed to help the genetic information coded in the DNA to utilize the ingredients to build a human body. We call this energy *Ki* (often spelled *Chi*). Ki is the basket that carries the information and the web that unites the material.

Three Bodies: Physical, Energy, and Spiritual

Material, energy, and spirit are the basic elements that make up our physical bodies and our existence itself. The phenomenon of life is the interplay of these three elements. Not only does human life consist of these elements, but so do the lives of every living thing that surrounds us. However, when we are trapped inside a world defined only by the five physical senses, we do not realize the energy and spiritual aspects of life. All we recognize is the material phenomenon. We call this the physical body.

The first body, the physical, can be seen and touched. This is the body experienced with the world of the five senses. When our bodies are supremely relaxed yet our awarenesses alert, we can feel an energy field that surrounds our bodies. This energy field permeates and envelopes us. Some people can actually see this field of energy. This is the energy body. The third body, the spiritual, cannot be sensed by the five senses. We cannot touch, smell, see, feel, or hear the spirit. Our existence here and now is a phenomenon or an output of various aspects of spirit as expressed in this particular time and space; information itself is not subject to the limitations of time or space. Absolute freedom, infinite existence—these terms refer to the sphere of the spirit.

The highest plane of activity in the phenomenon of life is information generation. If information is created, then material substance comes into being to actualize the information. The spiritual body can be said to consist of pure information. In fact, the spiritual body is analogous, in a way, with the "information body." An example of this could be this book, a dance, or a musical performance, the act of building a house or inventing a toy, or forming an organization such as a company or nation. In fact, everything that you want to do or have ever wanted to do has been a product of new or recycled information. By generating information, you are creating the conditions under which your life exists. The process of generating information and putting it into realization can be called "creation." You are a creator.

See how multifaceted you are? From chemical compounds to creator? Which part of this grand process would you single out to define your life? Since everything is a process of life, which part would you choose to call "living?" Furthermore, on which part of this process would you place the worth of life? In other words,

19

would you regard one aspect of the life process as more worthy of being called "life" than another?

No matter what our choices are, and regardless of our understanding of it, life will continue to exist. However, depending on how narrowly we set the limits of a definition, life can be many things to many people. Life can mean that the heart beats and blood flows. Life can mean that the brain is functioning and you are processing information. So, depending how we choose to define life, our definitions and attitude toward death are also consequently varied.

Let's take the example of injury. What does it mean? Does it mean bruises and black-and-blue marks? Does it mean a cut in the skin? How about injuries to the energy and spiritual bodies? If your spiritual body is healthy, then your energy body is healthy, leading to the self-healing of a physical injury. But what if your spiritual body is damaged? The damage to the spiritual/information body does not only mean that your genetic information is damaged. The genetic information is only a minuscule part of the information that makes up who you are. The worst damage that the spiritual/information body can sustain is planting wrong ideas of identity and twisted standards of value in it.

Factors that Threaten the Spiritual/Information Body

If you live entirely within a limited field of information, you do not have the vision and ability even to realize that you live within this limitation. If you are unknowingly trapped inside an elevator that is falling at great speed, you will not realize your own entrapment until you can look out a window and realize that the walls are zooming by. Someone who is limited by societal conventions can only act in ways that reflect his or her limitations, no matter how hard he might try to break free of the limitations.

The ideology of freedom itself is just a piece of information. Do you think that people were not "free" before the ideologies of freedom, fairness, equality, and religion came into being? Before religion, didn't people have a notion of salvation, or enlighten-ment, or sin? The words "freedom" and "salvation" did not herald the actual ideas of freedom or salvation; these existed long before. In fact, the invention of words or terms to denote an idea or a state of being could push us farther away from experiencing the quali-ties they evoke.

I said earlier that enlightenment is a choice to break the illu-sion of grandeur that surrounds the concept. If pieces of informa-tion such as enlightenment, salvation, and freedom, all recognized for their positive contribution to human history, can be used to obfuscate the actual ideas behind them, how much more damage can negative information, such as the things that elicit guilt and fear, do to us?

Our spiritual/information body is exposed without any defense to the negative information that floats around us, polluting and injuring us. Any damage to the information body will twist our lives, our injuries are expressed through wrongful actions, putting us in danger, along with society and the world at large. How can you judge the severity of phenomena in which a piece of negative information can forever cripple a human soul and imprison it in a spiritual Alcatraz? Cripple and imprison not just one individual but billions of humans?

We don't realize that we are constantly being bombarded by negative information. We don't realize that our spiritual/informa-tion bodies are handicapped and imprisoned. Our recognition and judgment are twisted because the information body is damaged. Our thoughts are not free because our information bodies are imprisoned. The problem is all the more serious because we don't know we are in prison. We don't recognize bars as bars. We think that our information handicap is a matter of "morality" or "ethical superiority," justifying the condition so that we don't sense the inconvenience of our handicap. However, when bearers of handi-capped or damaged information come into contact with one another, each tries to maintain its justification at the expense of the other, inevitably leading to conflict. Witness the religious and ideological conflicts around the world today.

Aside from organized information such as religion and ideologies, there are countless pieces of information in the world that damage our information bodies. We call a program code that damages a computer a virus. However, we do not recognize the existence of an unimaginable "information virus" that can traverse the world in a few seconds. All of humanity can be exposed to a piece of information almost simultaneously. Our information bodies are exposed to these countless pieces of information, and these tidbits of information are processed and expressed through the physical body. Such a phenomenon speaks to the need to deal with life not only on a physical plane but also on energy and spiritual planes, comprehensively and in totality.

A New Spiritual Civilization Demands a New Self-Identity

Taken as a whole, advancements in modern technology are reaching an extent that cannot be described as merely "advances in modern technology." They are significant enough to be considered a turning point in human history. Everything in our lives has become digitized into bits of information, marketed and sold like any consumer product we use every day. Information is wealth. A civilization based upon "hardware" is being transformed into one based on "software." What do these changes mean to us? Do these changes herald a shift from a material civilization to a more comprehensive one that takes into account the body-mind-spirit connection—in a word, a spiritual civilization? Or do we need something more to make that shift? What is meant by a spiritual civilization? Would a spiritual civilization demand that we place our identities on the Internet?

The digitization of information may be a precursor to a spiritual civilization, but it is not the entirety of a spiritual civilization in and of itself. The crux of the question is this: on which point do you place the value of a human life? What is the goal of the information that we generate so copiously? If the goal of the current flow of information is to add to the bottom line and enrich our society, then we are still living in a juvenile civilization of superficial materialism, despite brilliant advances in information processing technology capable of dealing with dizzying amounts of information.

To define "civilization" in simple terms, a civilization is the collection of tools and other things that make our lives more comfortable and bearable. Therefore, the basic characteristics of a civilization depend on how people define "life." When we define life only in physical terms and our value system reflects the limits of such a one-dimensional definition, then our civilization is a material civilization, no matter how advanced the technology. A civilization may boast amazing technological advances, enviable amounts of information, and proficient use of energy; however, if the ultimate beneficiary of the above is the physical body, then that civilization is a relatively limited civilization, despite its advanced expressions of achievement.

On a physical plane, we are separate units. On a physical plane, the truth that "We are all One" can be understood only on an abstract and hypothetical level. We realize that this tomato that we are eating in New York City could contain chemical compounds recycled from garbage dumps in China, whose exports of fertilizer could have been used by farmers in Mexico who then export their crops to the U.S. We know that everything on Earth is eventually recycled and reused. However, this form of "Oneness" is outside the immediate realm of physical experience.

On a physical plane, we do not have enough time or space to track down each and every chemical compound to prove to ourselves that we are indeed "One." Therefore, we feel ourselves separate from one another if we experience our lives only on a physical plane.

When sages say "We are all One," they are speaking about oneness in the realm of energy and information. As an energy body, you can communicate with an inanimate rock and receive a response. Your spiritual/information body is fast and free. What is the speed of a thought? The size of thought? It will be faster than the fastest and larger than the largest. It is not subject to time or

23

space. In fact, the information that makes you who you are contains the history of existence itself, and you are doing your part, adding more to it.

To understand ourselves as a spiritual/information body, we cannot stop at just understanding the contents of the information. Information is not the essence of the spiritual/information body, however contrary it may sound. Information is just a mere ripple on the surface of the essence of existence. This essence is the spontaneous generation of energy within a void, an infinity contained within a zero, cosmic energy and cosmic mind rolled into one.

The purpose of recognizing the spiritual/information body is to recognize this essence, the ultimate wellspring of creation. Through such recognition, we will realize that the physical body is just a tool used by "life." In this plane, there is no differentiation between life and death. Just as falling leaves in autumn are a natural and perfect expression of life, so is the sprouting of leaves in spring. It is all one continuous process. You can call the recognition of this "enlightenment." More importantly, a civilization based on such recognition is a spiritual civilization. Therefore, in a spiritual civilization, enlightenment is common sense.

New Symbol of Life: Brain and Information

Until now, human civilization has used the heart and blood as the chief symbols for life. This symbolism is so pervasive (and obvious) that no one ever thinks of raising a question about its relevance, but what are the preconceptions behind such symbolism? Such symbolism says that we equate life with our physical bodies. In other words, we think that life is the physical body, and a function of the physical body. But think for a moment if we consider life in the new paradigm of body, energy, and spirit. Such consideration becomes common sense. What would happen then?

In all probability, the term, "death," might disappear, or at least be defined differently. We would undergo a profound and fundamental shift in our attitudes toward death. Our death experience would become a much more relaxed and comfortable affair. It would not be a time of grief, but a precious time to share hard-won experience and information with others. We would have a much more mature cultural view of death. When we will arrive at this level of understanding about death, we will no longer strive ceaselessly and at any cost to maintain the life functions of a physical body while neglecting our energy and spiritual bodies. This does not have to do with the sacredness of life but with a larger question of the definition of life.

The chief symbolism of life will change under those circumstances, from the heart and blood to the brain and information. We will judge a person's life by the quality of constructive information that she produces. Simultaneous with a change in the definition of life, controversy about genetic cloning and other ethical problems generated by scientific advances will disappear. We may be able to interchange our body parts with impunity, but we will probably not even bother, for an action designed merely to prolong our hold over material possessions and the physical body would imply a dire and embarrassing lack of the essence of life. As we realign our currently materialistic value system to correspond more closely to a newly earned and deeper understanding of life, we will use Earth's resources with more care and distribute them more equitably.

Today's science can peer into the source of existence and replicate life. We are confused about how to use such technology and skill. We are like children who have stumbled upon something they cannot understand. We are in need of an evolution in spirit and consciousness to match the advances in technology and science.

Now we need to escape from the prison of information and limited awareness. We need to escape from a limited physical self-identity and overcome spiritual/informational obstacles such as the concepts of nationality, ethnicity, and religion. We now need to understand life on a more comprehensive and fundamental level and to use that understanding to engage in a discussion to plan an ideal life on Earth and to see how to help each other to achieve such a life. Healing society on a basic level is only possible when such an understanding of life can be agreed upon and acted on.

You must choose and act upon your choice. You must experience yourself in multi-dimensional ways and use these experiences to redefine yourself and your relationships with others. You must observe how you are affecting the spiritual/information bodies of those around. You must then make a conscious decision to heal your family and neighbors, but also society and the Earth. When we escape this informational prison of physical self-identity, we will realize that it was an illusion, all puff and smoke, one of our own making.

God Is Not an Object of Worship, but an Object of Use

One of the most puzzling and challenging questions in the history of humankind has been that of God. What is God? How do you define God? This is the question that led history's geniuses to the brilliant explanations and highest intellectual achievements, as well as the deepest experiences of despair. Differing answers to this question led to immeasurable suffering and it continues to be the cause of conflicts around the world today.

God Defines Our Limits and Our Hopes

We call the unknown "God." When human civilization was at its cradle, we called everything around us "gods." Every tree, rock, flowers, and leaves had a god watching over it. Behind every natural phenomenon such as rain, wind, and fire was a god. Dictating the whims of natural catastrophes was a capricious god, both feared and respected. We were surrounded by the unknown. We were surrounded by gods. As humans learned the workings behind each unknown, our "unknowns" became "knowns" and the gods' domain decreased in size.

However, as we expanded our field of knowledge, we also realized how much more there was to know. Our biggest realization was of our own ignorance. We realized that we did not know much. As our intellects grew, so did the realization of our ignorance. We still have many upon many questions: Why is the sky so endless and blue? Why are there so many stars in the cosmos? Who am I and why am I here? When we ask these fundamental questions, we still look to God. God represents the limitations of our knowledge. When our intellect ends, our God rules.

We also call the collection of our impossible hopes and dreams God. When we can attain something by ourselves, we do so. When we can't, we ask God to attain it for us. When we are thirsty and there is a spring within our reach, we don't ask God for water. However, when we are in the middle of a desert with nary a drop of dew in sight, or in the middle of a drought with Earth in tatters and crops in disarray, we pray to God for rain.

In such a fashion, God represents the sum of the wants that we cannot attain by ourselves. This is why God grew in importance as our wants and desires grew in strength. God's domain is the same size as the domain of our unattainable wants. When we want something that we cannot have, the energy of such a hope or want powers the realm of God. God represents the limit of our current ability to attain something. When our ability is lacking, God rules.

God's History: From Tribal Deities to God

Along with our wants and desires, our gods matured as our egos grew. When our awareness stopped at the tribal level, our gods were tribal gods. When our awareness expanded to include an ethnic identity, our gods were ethnic gods. Our gods grew through conquests. During tribal struggles, gods of war and gods of vengeance ruled the day. As our wants and desires grew, gods came to be more powerful and important, creating a divine hierarchy based upon power and strength.

Although gods grew in strength according to humanity's needs, individual gods retained their individual traits, formed when they first appeared on Earth. A god of anger still remains a god of anger, and a god of jealousy still turns green with envy. An ethnic god still practices preferential treatment toward its chosen people, although not so obviously as before.

Currently, many efforts are underway to create a unified, inter-connected world, although each effort has differing aims and goals. During this process, civilizations clash, traditions conflict, and understandings differ. Simply put, one type of information goes up against another. The war of gods continues.

Looking at it from an economic or technological point of view, the world is already a unified whole, with financial transactions completed on the Internet in a fraction of a second, without regard to countries or religions. However, from a cultural or traditional point of view, humanity is still living in units defined by nations or ethnic groups. Although there is an effort underway, such as in the European Commonwealth, to expand the traditional political boundaries, humanity has not been able to escape the prison of nationality when it comes to expanding cultural boundaries. As the Soviet experiment has shown, attempts to forcibly unify different cultures and nationalities come to an explosive head as soon as the controlling external force is eliminated.

The United States is perhaps the only successful example of different people living together as one national unit. The main reason for this success probably lies in that the U.S. never bothered to acknowledge or focus on the bewildering array of cultures represented by her citizens; instead, she built a society based upon an implied social contract that specified specific behavioral limits for all based on basic social values held in common by the founding majority. The Founding Fathers built a system in which only the most essential issues had to be agreed upon, the rest of the details being left to each person's own choice and expression.

Generally, unlike the U.S., the various human cultural traditions are still limited by nationality. So are our gods. Do you believe in a god? If so, find out the nationality of your god. The gods that we know today have their bases in specific nationalities.

We don't yet have a god that can represent Earth as whole. The various conflicts inflicted in the name of God or any god today speak to the limitations of the gods we believe in.

When the village represented the entirety of life, people thought that their god ruled that village. As their powers grew and territory expanded, people thought that their god ruled over all the territory they conquered. As people discovered more lands and new continents, along with colonialism and imperialism, the conquerors' gods came with them. When humanity finally realized the existence of Earth as a whole, people thought that their particular god should be the one to rule over Earth. They each used any and all means necessary to this end, the most common means being war.

Although there are always compound reasons for a war, something to do with the gods or God has been the most frontal and vocal reason. The majority of wars were fought in the name of God. The gods of the losers lost their rule and the winners' gods expanded their domain. However, although their domain expanded, they still remained within the confines of a nationality. Our gods, therefore, are fundamentally an expression of a national or group ego. Our gods mainly act to justify the injustices that are used to deliver profits and benefits to their respective peoples. A child's mind in the body of a destructive adult—this is the shape of our gods today, as entities without enough self-discipline to control their self-serving wants and needs.

Our gods are ourselves: self-serving, self-justifying, and self-centered. We were not made in a god's image; instead, that god was made in our image. Our "god" knows as much as we do; our "god" feels exactly how we feel. Our level of consciousness determines the level of our god's consciousness. A god of rage justifies our rage; a god of revenge justifies our revenge. Our god justifies our conquest of other people's land and culture, in addition to the destruction of their history, politics, and economy. We do all these in the name of a god. No matter how brutal our actions may be, or how unjustified, we feel proud, for we are doing "our god's" work. We say God told us to do it.

God is where our ignorance and our wants are, allowing us to escape responsibilities for the self-serving actions we perpetrate in the name of God. God is an expression of our irresponsibility and ignorance and self-serving needs. These are the names of God.

God Is Information

God as a single being is information. God represents the collection of good or desirable social values of a specific group or people, those values that provide the glue that holds people together. However, God is just a collection of information that is powerless to do anything until it is mated to hardware and charged with energy. God is software. The tools that God uses are our bodies, brains, and organizations. The energy is provided by our faith or belief. Our consciousness provides the energy and the permission for God to use our all to do His bidding. We proudly consider ourselves to be instruments of God's will.

However, what is wrought by God is not His will, but ours. It is our need for security and our desire for domination that are being realized. God is not using us; we are using God. We raise and worship God to use Him. We may not realize that we are doing so, or we may pretend that we don't know, but that is exactly what we are doing.

The two largest reasons that we cannot free ourselves from the information called God are fear and guilt. Both fear and guilt have their roots in our ignorance about death. We are afraid because we cannot know. If someone claims to have a special knowledge about death, then we automatically grant him a special place of honor or respect, granting authority without any evidence. But let us pause and think for a moment.

Who among us, six billion strong, has experienced death? Not a near-death experience, but real death? Of course, everyone eventually experiences death once in her life. But there is yet no way to share that experience with someone else. Have any of you reading these words experienced death? If you answer, "yes," then wake up, for you are mistaken. You are not dead yet. Generally, we do not understand death. More clearly, our level of understanding about death is at the level of ignorance.

If we don't know what death is, what are we afraid of? What we are afraid of is not death, but information (or the lack thereof) about death. We are afraid of the accepted interpretation or myths about death. We are actually afraid about our own ignorance about death, and out of this ignorance rises our fear. Our ignorance has a deeper source in our ignorance about life itself: "Who am I?" "Why am I here?" If we knew the meaning of life and were able to judge ourselves as natural phenomena in the cycle of life, our fear about death would have no room to stand in our lives.

Do you still not know what your life's purpose is, or think that you don't know? When do you think you will find out? If you don't know your life's purpose, who do you think is more qualified to know? If you don't know, no one, not even God, will know. Then how do you find the answer to the question that not even God knows? There is only one way: choice.

Your choice is your answer. Choose who you want to be and what your life's purpose is. Choose enlightenment and choose knowledge. It is through choice that we can escape from ignorance and fear. When we choose knowledge, we can formulate a different idea about death. When you choose to know and are ready to take responsibility for your choice, you no longer need a "god" to justify your choices and "god's will" no longer has the power to ensnare you in a web of guilt and fear. You will then be able to use the idea of God to achieve your choices.

God Is an Object of Use, Not of Worship

The worth of a piece of information is determined by the results it brings, not by the intent in which it was produced. The standard by which information is judged is its ability to solve problems. We use information as a tool to realize our intents and achieve our goals. If information is not suited to these needs, then we either modify or ignore it. However, there is one collection of information that has escaped such review for thousands of years. That is the collection of information called "God."

What type of help can "God," a human concept that consists of differing bits of information, give us in our hour of need? How can God help us solve the problems facing humanity today? How can God help us in achieving world peace and arresting the environmental destruction of Earth? How can God help us in healing ourselves, our society, and our Earth, recovering the original health and harmony? Is this information called God still useful to us in creating a future for humankind?

It is time to put the idea of God under review. We have to see which pieces of information that make up "God" are still good and which have passed their date of expiration. We have to throw away the gods that still exist to create conflicts, desire revenge and destruction, and demand blind obedience and control. We have to throw away the masks of universality from those gods who claim to be for all people and expose them to their own reality as gods for a specific group or people, no longer useful to us as the whole of humanity. And if we find a god that is truly valuable to us, then we will reinstate its position and use it to our own ends. This process signifies a new discovery of social values and standards necessary to build a global village, not only of technology and economy, but of civilization: a human civilization.

God is information. However, there are two types of information. Let's make a computer analogy. If you want to produce a document, you use a program for word processing. Your document, as well as the word processor, is a collection of information. One is document information and the other is program information, used to create more information in the form of documents. God is like the word processor. God is a tool for creation, to be used but not worshipped. When you give yourself to God and let God use your brain and body, you are in fact letting the word processor run the computer and the user. When you become the master of the computer and use its many programs according to your will, then you become a conscious user. However, when you let the program run you, instead of the other way around, then you are a kind of ghost user, there, but not there. You become a slave to the information. Although this information can be of political or social ideology or religious dogma, you are a slave, nonetheless.

Although you need both hardware and software for the act of creation, it is up to you to choose what you will create and what programs and machines you will use. If the current software/hardware setup is not appropriate to what you seek to create, then you have to change it. You have to choose another system. This is your choice and responsibility as a conscious user of your own life.

Who are you? Who do you wish to be? Why do you live? Why do you want to live? The answers to these questions are all choices you make. You can use "God" to actualize these choices, for God is a tool you use to create your life. In the midst of this creation, look into yourself and realize that you are the master of the information that you wield, that you are the master of your own life, and that you are the Creator.

5th ENLIGHTENMENT

A Fair Transaction—
Recovering the Zero Point

If you were an ancient king who unified many different and small nations into one great nation, what would you do first to make sure that the new country ran smoothly without internal squabbles? What would be the most urgent and necessary step? Use your imagination. Think.

Why Pounds and Kilograms Are Important

Historically, what the wise kings did after conquering a new territory was to decree that only one system of measurements be used in all future transactions. For example, you could only use kilos and meters when before you used pounds and feet. The king considered it crucial that he provide consistency in measurements. Why was this so important?

When forcibly joining together two previously separate countries into one nation, it is important for the leaders to plant an idea of a common nation and shared destiny among the people. Otherwise, differences will eventually fester and rend the nation asunder. Of course, these things take time. Most conflicts between people arise not out of some differences in culture or philosophy of life, but out of unfair or unjust everyday transactions. Unless you have to live with the person everyday, it is possible to turn a blind eye to another person's peculiar habits and mannerisms. However, to be cheated in a commercial transaction can cause an immediate conflagration of temper and resentment. This is as true now as it was two thousand years ago.

This is why wise kings of old, in order to establish a social order, made all units of measurements consistent. Fairness in transaction begins with measurements; in a word, the kings wanted to introduce fairness in all transactions. If every merchant had his own different balances and weights, it would create chaos and inevitably lead to fights and bloodshed.

Even today, different parts of the world use different units of measurement and worth. The U.S. still insists on using the mile and pounds while the rest of the world, with some exceptions, uses the metric system. However, since the conversion between the two systems is accurate and universally accepted, there is no source of conflict except for the cumbersome calculation required. The same goes for currency, with each country having its own system of money. Such differences in units of measurements are not sources of conflict in the world.

What is a cause for conflicts and arguments is the different *value* that each person places upon the same thing. Even if a "Mickey D's Quarter-Pounder" is a quarter-pounder whether measured in kilograms or pounds, each person and each society places different worth on the same amount of hamburger. This is because each person and each society has different standards by which they measure value. Until now, we considered such differences to be a matter of fact, obvious and ubiquitous.

Meaning of a Transaction and Limits of a Market System

The market has been the system through which different values came together and formed a compromise. A product's worth is decided by its demand and supply, and is dealt with according to the value decreed upon it by the market. If a certain product is popular, its price goes up accordingly, and more effort and money are invested into making it. Such is the basic law of the market system. However, we are stumped to explain certain phenomena that do not follow the supply-and-demand model, and we are coming to realize the inherent limitations of this market system.

One of the underlying assumptions is that every person is informed fully and equally about the relevant information that could have a bearing on a certain product. However, we know that such an assumption is unrealistic. Even worse, a fatal flaw in the market system is that life's most basic values are not "priceable" and therefore not available for transactions in a market. Our current market system is neither mature enough to deal with such values, honest enough to acknowledge that such values exist, nor detailed enough to transact such values.

There are cases in which a supplier does not participate in the market system for one reason or another and is prevented from being paid an equitable value for his products. There are also cases in which a transaction is not considered a transaction because of dishonesty or corruption. For example, if biodiversity is considered crucial to maintaining a stable ecosystem, what is the market value of a species? What about the market value of a clean environment, which everyone agrees is essential to the survival of the human species? What is the market value of a new global epistemology that will lead Earth into a healthy twenty-first century? What is the market value of salvation and immortality as promised in religions? How much would you pay for enlightenment?

All these are transactions. Our life is a series of transactions. Market transactions are just a minuscule part of the everyday information/energy transactions that we engage in. There are many methods of payment for these transactions. We can pay with money; we can pay with effort. A thoughtless action can become a lingering burden, while a kind smile can melt away the debt of several lifetimes. You can pay in one lump sum, or pay in installments. You can pay the price as marked, or you can negotiate. You can use donations as payments. Despite the dizzying choices of forms of payment, these are all transactions. You have to pay, in some way or another, now or later, for what you have bought.

To consider everything in life as a transaction does not make it "unspiritual." In fact, not admitting a transaction to be a transaction is immature and hypocritical. How many different types of transactions can our current market system deal with? If our market system was of sufficient maturity and sophistication to be able to deal with all forms of transactions fairly, giving people an exact value for the choices that they make or are about to make, then we would no longer need the cosmic "payment system" that we often call karma.

The market system is a brilliant and equitable system of determining the value of a product according to the prevailing conditions at the time of the transaction, and it is a good system for dealing with products that can be assigned a value in this way. However, some things cannot be assigned a value through a normal market process because they lack a central standard of value. The market does not have a central standard of value that can encompass everything that can be transacted. We are talking about the Euro or the U.S. dollar. We are talking about a central standard of value that everyone can agree upon beforehand, and against which the values of all products, whether material, information, or ideas, can be judged. What if such a central standard of value existed?

Colored Glasses and a Scale

The problem of a central standard of value takes us to the philosophical question of epistemology or knowing. The fact that we place differing values on the same object says that we recognize things in varying ways. Even deeper, what is meant by "knowing" and/or "recognizing"? How do we know what we know? Do we, as humanity, share a common recognition for certain things? How can we confirm this common sharing?

If a rose were in front of us right now, you and I would both recognize it as a rose. I would describe its color as red, and you, in all likelihood, would do the same. However, does that mean that this rose looks exactly the same to me as it does to you? Let's assume, for a moment, that I am wearing blue-tinted glasses and you are wearing yellow-tinted ones. Imagine that we don't know that we are wearing these tinted glasses because we have been wearing them for such a long time that we no longer are aware of wearing them. Maybe we never were. Not only us, but our teachers and parents wore these tinted glasses.

However, you and I could agree that the rose is red because we have been trained to define the color of the rose as red, even though we might be registering two different colors as they come to us through our differently colored lenses. This shows that the color red in my realm of knowledge could be a different color than in your world. If we could enter another person's brain, we might be surprised to learn that what I think of as the color red is different from what another person thinks of as red. You might find yourself exclaiming, "I always thought his red was my blue!" What color lens do your glasses have? Is it possible to see an object with objectivity?

The way we recognize or see an object is like using a scale. Each person is using his own scale to weigh an object. Accordingly, everyone will have a different weight for the same object. This is akin to us seeing the same object in different ways. Why is that? Are these scales imperfect? No, there is nothing wrong with the scales. It's possible, right now, to see that there is nothing wrong with our internal scales. Lean your body to one side. When it is leaning to one side, ask yourself who is really you. Are you the one who is leaning or the one who recognizes that the body is leaning? Let us change the question. Is your recognition perfect? If not, are you the one whose recognition is imperfect, or the one who knows that her recognition is imperfect? How you do know that your recognition is imperfect?

The reason that we know the imperfectness of our recognition is due to the inherent "perfectness" of our inner knowledge.

Whether you know it or not, there exists within you a grain of "perfect" knowledge, not as a result of some effort on your part, but as an inherent gift to all human beings. This core of perfect knowledge is enlightenment, and it is your choice to recognize it or not. This core is the basis for all recognition. This is what I mean when I say that there is no flaw in our internal scale.

Why, then, do we see the same object in different ways? Why do our scales read different weights for the same object? It is not because your scale is off, but because your scale is not calibrated to "zero." Why is your scale not calibrated to "zero"? The answer is simple. There is already something on it.

We have put something on the scale and forgotten to take it off. In other words, the reason that we all have different standards of value is not because our scales our flawed, but because our scales have a weight already on them. Each individual has a different weight on his scale. Since the internal scale is perfect, it faithfully reflects the different weights that we, as individuals, place upon it. This is why, when we place the same object upon the scales, the readings are all off by the weight of the objects already lying on top of the scales. We just don't remember or recognize that we have placed this burden there. It's akin to wearing a pair of tinted glasses without knowing it.

It is not necessary for the scale to always point to zero, nor is it necessary to look at everything without tinted glasses. The problem lies in forgetting to take the weight off the scales and in not remembering you have glasses on. If we could remember to go back to the zero reading on the scales, there would be no problem whatsoever. Enlightenment is not maintaining the zero reading at all times; enlightenment is the perfect internal scale itself. Of course, it is up to individual choice if one wants to maintain the zero state of his scale by living alone in some cave or on a mountaintop, but it is not necessary to become enlightened. No. All you have to do is to be able to recognize that you are wearing colored glasses and know you have something pressing down on the scale—and to be able to take off the glasses and the weight.

As long as we are in this physical form, we have to eat, excrete, sleep, and engage in social relationships. Every moment of your life is a series of choices, and to make a choice, you have to judge your situation beforehand. You have to weigh the situation on your internal scale. Then you have to take responsibility for the choices that you make. Although everyone starts with their scales at zero, we put so much stuff on them as we live that we eventually forget what we have on the scales, and lose our sense of the zero.

Central Standard of Value: Earth

How can we restore the zero reading? What is meant by restoring the zero reading? This process of restoration is a purely subjective experience. You cannot restore your state of zero by looking at someone's else's scale. No, you have to reawaken your own sensitivity, pay off your "debts," and recover your own zero. In the context of everyday life, in everyday society, recovering the zero means that you have a correct value system as a guide to your actions, a value system that can fairly and equitably judge all other values. What could be the central standard of value that could embrace the diverse values of the world and promote understanding and co-existence among them?

Until now, we humans have celebrated ourselves as the final arbitrators of all living things on Earth and we have organized our world accordingly. We have dealt with others and the Earth under the premise that we are separate individuals, at war with one another and the world, surviving through ceaseless competition, our standards of value always at the whim of our ever-changing emotions and moods. Such has been the limit of our value system. Such is the life that we lead today.

If human beings are too subjective and "full of themselves" to develop an objective criterion for values, then what about natural sciences, religions, or politics? How does science define truth? Even in the supposedly objective realm of natural sciences, most people agree that the standards of truth only go as far as the paradigm currently in vogue among the majority of scientists. All religions that purport to teach the everlasting truth and the gods that they uphold have, despite claims of universality, specific prejudices for a certain nation or people, causing conflicts and fights. We don't yet have a single representative God of Earth.

How about the concepts of justice and freedom, whose pursuit is lauded as a universal human trait? Freedom fights against freedom, and justice strikes against justice. This is because even freedom and justice are subject to the subjective interpretation of a particular group. This is fighting between information as produced by the tinted lenses of different groups. Original freedom and justice have no conflicts within them. Everything, including so-called universal truths of natural sciences, religions, and politics, is trapped within the cage of the prevailing paradigm.

How much time did it take for human beings, descendants of monkeys but with an advanced intellectual potential, after making their appearance on Earth and wondering at the mysteries of the stars, Moon, and Sun, to realize they were not at the center of the known cosmos? In the beginning, it was probably humiliating and absolutely terrifying to relinquish the notion that the universe revolved around them. But now, it is evidence of the maturity of human awareness. Now it's time to once again present evidence for our continuing growth. We need another Copernican Revolution in the collective human consciousness. What we need now is to realize that humanity is not the center of Earth and to find the real center of the natural harmony. That center of harmony is the Earth, not human beings.

The central standard of value for our life here on Earth should be Earth Herself, not our egos, needs, wants, and prejudices. We can use Earth as the standard by which to judge all actions on Earth. From such a point of view, we all become Earth-Humans first, before we are a part of a group, nation, or religion.

If there were no Earth, then no altars could exist for you to worship your god. You wouldn't exist, nor your god. Without Earth, no nation would exist, nor would political ideologies with which to rule a nation. With eternal hope, we may eventually all learn to recover the zero point and become one with the cosmic consciousness. However, before that happens, it is more crucial that we attain an Earth consciousness. To do so, we need to overcome the group egotism that binds us, knowingly or unknowingly. All our choices and actions should be judged by the effects they have on Earth. All our choices should be geared to empty the scale of Earth and return it to zero. That is the reward and the responsibility of our choices. From zero to zero—this is the expression of the grand cycle of the cosmos.

The Meaning of the Recovery of the Zero

As long as we are alive, we have to act, which involves an endless series of choices. Our choices always churn the waters of equanimity and harmony into chaos. It is the actions of Ki and *Tao* to calm the waters and return them to original harmony. In this sense, Tao, which means the "Way" in a literal translation, is the force for the Original Order in the universe, a cosmic rubber band that always returns to its original shape even after undergoing myriad transformations and changes. The process of living always creates chaos, and the flow of Tao tames the chaos. Responsibility not only becomes an act of accepting the consequences of your choices, but also the act of recovering the harmony, the original state of zero. If we were to borrow an analogy from physics, this principle would best be represented by entropy, the Second Law of Thermodynamics. Karma is also another expression of this principle of recovering the original state of zero.

Recovering the zero does not mean that everything disappears and nothing remains. Your experience remains. If you are wise, you would use this experience to fertilize and nurture soul. In addition to gaining self-confidence and respect for others, you would gain deep inner peace. This is the true meaning of maturity.

We all learned in kindergarten to put a toy back in its place once we are done playing with it. What the child gets out of playing with a toy is not the toy itself, nor the temporary emotional delight, but the maturity he gains from the experience. If the child seems too attached to the toy and refuses to let it go, then we recognize it as a worrisome sign of possible emotional or mental disturbance. In like manner, as a society, we are currently too attached to the "toy" and not to the lesson that playing may impart to further the maturation of our collective soul.

I recall seeing a sign in a national park. It read, "Please take with you what you brought and leave what was here already." This should be the basic axiom when dealing with Earth. Earth is not ours to do with as we please. We have just been granted temporary stewardship of Earth. We did not purchase Earth with money. What we can attain during our time on Earth is not more land or higher skyscrapers but maturity. We have been granted permission to use the grand "toy," the whole of the natural environment, as a tool to facilitate our maturity. This is why we have a responsibility to return the toy to its rightful place in its original condition.

Such awareness should be the basic minimum that guides our actions. If we base politics and economics upon this minimum, then politics become Earth-Politics and economics becomes Earth-Economics. When this minimum becomes the ruling policy of the land, we will no longer need the system of karma and reincarnation introduced solely for the purpose of us paying off our debts.

In order to engage in a fair and equitable transaction, we have to acknowledge first that our inner scales are perfect; second, that they are not calibrated to zero because we have put something on them and forgotten to take it off; third, that Earth can provide the central standard of value that can unify and embrace all the diverse values of the world; and fourth, that we have a responsibility to make choices that allow us to return everything to its original zero state. This is the enlightenment of an Earth-Human and the life of an Earth-Human.

If we all learn to calibrate our scales to zero, then fair and orderly transactions are possible, not only with each other, but also with the Earth and the Heavens. When enough scales are calibrated correctly, transactions in information and material will occur fairly and equitably, leading to a world of harmony and peace. To do this, we must all see if the needles on our scales point to zero, and embrace an Earth-Human awareness. When such awareness becomes the basic human awareness, then we will have established a global village.

6th ENLIGHTENMENT

There Are No Chosen People

Once upon a time, a famous and respected teacher gave one of his students a piece of candy and said, "I am giving this especially to you." Deeply touched, the student did not know what to do. He hid the candy in his closet, as he would a treasure, to ensure that no one saw it, lest they steal it, although no one in the school would have stolen a piece of candy. The next day, the teacher called together all the students and gave each one of them a piece of the same type of candy, as an encouragement to study more. The student who had first received the candy felt his body go lax with disappointment, and he felt a keen rage of betrayal. The teacher had made his "specialness" disappear. He was now like everyone else.

The Desire to Become Special

From individual fashion expressions to the marketing strategy of multi-national conglomerates, the desire to be special, to stand out, must be one of the strongest motivating forces in our current society. Such motivations have, it must be admitted, driven some individuals, organizations, and even countries to develop faster and advance further than others. However, this type of growth is based on differentiating and separating oneself from others. It carries a serious risk to life as a whole and must, therefore, be reexamined.

This relative "specialness" is not just a matter of freedom of individual expression. It carries the unmistakable scent of competition that spirals ever upwards. All expressions of life are already special by definition. Every flower is beautiful. The specialness of life is absolute and not subject to a relative comparison. The beauty of a rose cannot be judged inferior nor superior to the beauty of a butterfly. They are both beautiful and special. Then why do we insist on standing out by comparing ourselves to others? What is the basic compelling force behind the drive to become special? It is the craving for attention that comes from the need for recognition. Turned inside out, it is the twisted expression of an ego with an inferiority complex.

One of the most serious symptoms of this "Chosen Syndrome" is the mistaken belief that God has especially chosen one. This problem becomes most serious and dangerous when a group or nation, sharing a common heritage, believes that it is the chosen of God. It is dangerous because such a belief can easily justify the conquest of other people's lands, property, and way of life. The God of such a chosen people does not represent a universal truth, but is a twisted manifestation of the collective ego of a group or nation. Unfortunately, most of the gods that humanity worships today have had their start in such a fashion, choosing one people over another and ensuring the success of the chosen at the suffering and expense of the other. Our gods are gods of superiority.

From an anthropological point of view, the Chosen Syndrome would be considered a natural phenomenon. Since our gods are originally all nationalistic or ethnocentric gods, whom would they single out to be special other than the people whose collective ego the gods represent in the first place? Who would your ego choose as special other than yourself? Just as naturally, there is nothing terribly wrong about a group or a nation declaring itself special. However, one thing that we have to realize is that this is a self-declaration of specialness and not an objective designation by the universal and everlasting truth of the cosmos. The cosmos has not declared one group superior to another.

As I wrote before, a god is an amalgam of good social values of a specific group or people. Therefore, God is a set of information used by this group to determine the desirability of a certain action or idea in a particular place and time. Since God is, by definition, a representation of a specific group, it cannot become the central standard of value that can unify Earth. Our information and distribution infrastructure is at a point in technological sophistication where it can unify the world under one system.

However, we are still far away from having a collective social value infrastructure that can bring the world under one umbrella. In other words, we don't have a chief Earth deity. We just have many smaller gods who are trying to bite off too big a piece of Earth for them to chew. The Chosen Syndrome is merely an expression of this sad reality.

What kind of constructive contribution can such an ethnocentric and nationalistic value system, as represented by the Chosen Syndrome, make toward the healing of society and the Earth? The value of a piece of information is in its ability to solve a problem. Information, whether it be a god or religion, must be upgraded or deleted and exchanged if it does not help us in solving problems. This is doubly true if that information is actually the cause of the problem.

The Meaning of Becoming an Earth-Human

What we need now is a value system that places Earth at its center. What we need now is an Earth-encompassing awareness. We are Earth-Humans. Before we are Americans, Japanese, or French, we are Earth-Humans. Before we are Christians, Buddhists, or Muslims, we are Earth-Humans. Just as we represent ourselves as Korean, American, or Mexican in an international forum, on a cosmic stage we have to represent ourselves as an Earth-Humans. Imagine that you arrived in an alien planet populated by intelligent aliens. When these aliens ask you where you are from, are you going to answer, "I am from New York"?

Our way of life already shows us that we are each Earth-Humans. Our communications and business transactions prove our lives as Earth-Humans. Do you still think that you only belong to one unit of organization, a nation or religion or company? Do you believe that any other organization is inherently foreign to the one to which you belong? Do you think you derive your self-identity from your membership in that organization?

The organizational units such as nation-state and ethnic group are remnants of our past habits and do not apply to our new way of life. Becoming an Earth-Human means you break out of a self-imposed idea of who you are and embrace the reality of who you are. Originally, there was only one Earth. This is still true. All other boundaries are artificial and exist for convenience's sake only. These traditional boundaries are quickly being left behind by the current reality of the world. The Earth-Human is no longer a conceptual idea—it is already our reality.

So, what does becoming an Earth-Human mean? What does it mean to love Earth as an Earth-Human? Just as the love of a country does not mean only the love of the territory, the love of Earth does not only mean environmental concern and activism. Loving Earth means that you recognize yourself as a member of the Earth community. Just as a father will care for his family and a citizen will show loyalty to one's country, an Earth-Human will do his all to fulfill his responsibility and role in the Earth community, deriving happiness and pleasure from such a life.

When we all accept and embrace an Earth-based value system, all the conflicts and differences that came from disagreements among the smaller value systems of the world will disappear. When we all become Earth-Humans, religious differences will be a matter of individual taste and ideological disagreements will only add to the peaceful diversity of opinions. In an Earth-Community, these differences will no longer cause conflicts, but will merely represent cultural diversity and richness.

We don't have to learn or prepare something special to become an Earth-Human. All we need is first, the recognition that our current sense of self-identity and the associated system of supporting beliefs and information are no longer relevant; and second, the choice to step out this shell just as you would throw away a shirt that no longer fits.

This does not mean that you have to feel scorn or resentment for your old sense of self. Do you feel angry at the clothes you threw away as a kid because they no longer fit? No, those clothes protected you and served their role well when they still fit you. It's just that you don't need those clothes anymore because you have grown up. It is perfectly natural to discard the clothes that don't fit because you grew out of them. It is unnatural to insist on wearing children's clothing when you are an adult. In the same manner, becoming an Earth-Human does not mean you throw away anything nor does it mean that you become something entirely new. Becoming an Earth-Human merely means that you come into your natural self.

To Earth, humanity is not everything. If humans were to disappear tomorrow, there are countless life forms that would gladly continue to inhabit Earth. Earth has her own life to maintain and keep. When Earth feels that She is being put into serious danger, She will have to make a choice to protect Herself, for the beauty and richness of Earth is far too precious to the cosmos for it to be destroyed by the self-destructive tendencies of a race of glorified monkeys. We have to recognize we are part of the life of Earth. Earth is not ours to do with as we please. We are Hers. We belong to Her. To Earth, we are all Earth-Humans, regardless of color, religious beliefs, or citizenship. To Earth, we are just another addition to the incredible array of life forms on Her land, in an endless cycle of biodiversity. To Earth, there is absolutely no reason why one religion or one people is better than another. To Earth, there are no chosen people.

7th ENLIGHTENMENT

Birth Is Not a Blessing

Five babies are born on the Earth every second. Half of them die before they reach the age of five. Even if they survive, life for most of them will be a series of hardships, with anxiety and fear dogging their every step. How was your birth? Your life thereafter? Do you think your birth was a blessing? If so, what are your reasons?

What about death, then? Do you think death is a blessing also? If you think that death is a misfortune, then how can you consider the event that eventually leads to death a blessing? If there were no birth, there would be no death. Our brains cells start to die off as soon as we take our first lungful of air. Aging and dying start as soon as we are born. Ironically, we consider death a great misfortune, but regard birth, the prerequisite event, to be a great blessing.

Happiness that Goes beyond Happiness

"Happiness is a state of mind." "Choose to be happy." "Create your own happiness." We have heard these and similar sayings so many times that they are almost clichés. Let us ask a more basic question: Why do you seek to be happy? Why do you put forth such an effort to be happy?

"Life has a meaning." "I am a good person." "My life is a worthy life." "I am happy." "I create my own happiness." Why do we need so many self-motivational maxims? After spending your whole day in the never-ending pursuit of happiness, have you ever gone to bed wishing that life could be over as soon as possible? Real happiness is not generating conditions that can produce happiness, but being free from the pounding pressure to always be happy. Real happiness is going beyond the constant *need* to be happy.

1st Insight: Life Is Suffering

In order to gain the freedom referred to previously, you need to gain an insight into three basic truths of life. The first insight is that life is suffering. Birth is suffering, as well as eating, drinking, loving, parting, coming together, drifting apart—all these are forms of suffering. Forget about the things we actually admit to be suffering; even the things that we define as joyful create stress for us in that they take us away from a state of equanimity.

If birth is a blessing and life a source of continuous happiness, then we don't need spiritual maturity or enlightenment, for when you are happy, you look for a continuation of that happiness. But you are not looking for something else, something better. When you look for something else, you feel a lack of something in your current reality. We try to solve a problem only when we perceive a problem, and we try to fill a space only when we see that it's empty.

When a person is happy, she does not ask for a reason. She is satisfied in just being happy. When you are happy, you dance, sing, and laugh; you don't think about the deeper meaning of life. A Buddha may laugh, but not a philosopher, for joy and happiness are contrary to the motivation to philosophize. In a happy country, should such a place ever exist, all philosophers would be unemployed.

We start asking about the meaning of life when conditions that produced our happiness disappear or when we realize that such conditions never last for long. At this juncture, we start asking questions: Why is this happening to me? What point is there to life? But when we are surrounded by happiness again, we forget about these questions and go merrily along our way. When "happy" conditions disappear once more, we start asking the same questions again, such as "How can this happen to me again?" When we have finally become jaded and distrustful of this thing called happiness, when we have finally seen happiness as the illusion that it really is, our questions start becoming more urgent: Who am I? Why was I born? Where did I come from? Where am I going?

As our questions become deeper, we start stripping off the layers of meaning that we had so carefully constructed around our lives, a process that leads to emptiness and loneliness. Most of us cannot bear this loneliness, and try our best to forget about the questions, yet we remain haunted always by their echoes in the back of our minds. However, if we wish to realize the truth behind life, we need the courage to look this emptiness straight in the eye. When you have realized that life is basically suffering punctuated by fleeting moments of happiness, when you are caught in that state of unbearable emptiness, you need courage and discipline to hold on to the questions that cry out from the depth of your soul. When you find yourself wishing, with all your being, to search for the unchanging truth, then you have taken that first step toward true freedom.

2nd Insight: My Body Is Mine, But It Is Not Me

The second insight that you need to experience is that your body is yours, but not you. My body is mine, but it is not me. When you feel yourself slighted and angry, when you feel your life is a sad joke, take a moment and ask who is this "me" who was slighted. You will realize that this "me" is a product, much like an appliance, packaged with various features such as age, job, religion, and hobbies. The "me" who was slighted is just a collection of information that you have gathered along the way. All the happiness, sadness, anger, and joy are generated by the mistaken assumption that your physical form is you. You are not unhappy. A phenomenon called the body and the layers of information that clothe it feel happy, sad, angry, or joyful. However, your body is never you, though it is yours.

What does this mean? If my body is not me but it is mine, who is the "me" that calls this body its own? If the entity that experiences my everyday life is just a phenomenon of a physical manifestation sheathed by layers of information, what is the real "me"?

To know that "my body is mine, not me" signifies that you know who the true master of your life is. The "me" that you have known throughout your life is just a collection of information that you started accumulating just after you were born. Your religious faith and your God are just a part of the information shell that you have constructed around yourself. Information did not cause your existence. Information started to form a shell around you after you were born, and this shell will disappear just before your body dies. It is akin to the programs inside a computer: all programs are closed before the computer turns itself off.

This collection of information changes faster than your body. Although your body shape and your physical abilities change over time, they don't change as quickly as your mind. Have you ever thought about how fickle your feelings of self-worth are? One moment, you are King of the World, a truly magnificent person. The next minute, you are in despair with feelings of inadequacy and weakness. You are full of life's meaning and motivation one second, but succumb to despair and emptiness the next. If your body changed sizes as capriciously as your mind, you would change your clothes thousands of times a day. That is how unstable and fleeting information is.

Observe your body. It breathes. You breathe when you are asleep, when you are no longer conscious of your own ideas of self-identity. Who, then, is breathing? The collection of information that you mistakenly think is you is not the main protagonist in the activity of the breath. In fact, *you* are not breathing; breath naturally happens in you. You can purposely end your life, but you cannot purposely keep your life going. The expression, "my life" is actually an oxymoron, a result of ignorance and mistaken assumption. You don't possess life; life expresses itself through you. Your body is a flower that life let bloom, a phenomenon created by life.

When you say, "My body is mine, but not me," you have realized that the real "me" is a self-perpetuating, eternally existing process/entity called life. You can call it the Tao, true self, nature—it doesn't matter. It exists without your understanding, beyond the realm of your information. It exists by itself, for itself, and of itself. When you say, "My body is mine, but not me," you have realized who's the true master of your breath, your life. I would like to call this realization "meeting the divinity within." This is the second insight.

Life is suffering. Birth is suffering. As long as you are mired in the illusion that your body is you, life cannot be anything else but an endless cycle of suffering and pain. To know that life is suffering alleviated only by intense moments of happiness, is the first insight. To realize that a spark of divinity exists within you, in midst of suffering and emptiness, is the second insight.

3rd Insight: Hope Leads to the Perfection of the Soul

The vast majority of people end their lives trapped in ignorance and fear, without coming across the first insight. They end their physical lives without knowing where they came from or where they are going, grasping hungrily at empty things until the last possible moment, only to realize with the last gasp of their breath that life is empty suffering. With their dying breaths, they may catch a glimpse of the divinity within, but, alas, all they can see at that point is the back of the divinity as it leaves. Only a very few people meet the divinity within when they are alive. However, knowing that divinity exists and expressing divinity in reality are two different things. The third insight is needed to actualize the divinity within that you have been so fortunate to discover.

The key to making the divinity bloom is hope, the same hope that forces an endless fountain of energy to shoot forth from within us. I call this a "vision." A vision is a spiritual business plan in which you lay out the strategy and actions through which you intend to actualize the divinity you have discovered. Vision is life's goal that you have created through your choice to be enlightened. A soul becomes perfected through vision. Your divinity becomes complete only when you throw everything into achieving the vision.

A vision is not a pie in the sky. A vision is: one, good enough to make your face shine with joyful light when you think about it; two, fulfilling enough to provide you with an untiring motivation; three, attractive enough to deserve all your concentration and energy; four, useful enough to gain the appreciation of those around you; and five, concrete and clear enough so that everyone can determine whether you have succeeded. These are the basic conditions to a vision. Because of the vision, and because the vision is alive and dynamic, we can continue on the road to divine perfection, despite moments of fatigue and difficulty.

To actualize your divinity through your vision may be a matter of choice, but it also can be a matter of situation, because a vision is created not for self-satisfaction but for the purpose of sharing your enlightenment with others. Say a flower recognized itself as a flower and bloomed forth in all its glory; however, if this flower did not have anyone who could appreciate its beauty and with whom it could share its fragrance, then what good would this flower be in such a place? We are fortunate. We are blessed with a situation in which we can fully use our abilities to heal society and Earth.

To know that physical life is suffering, to know that your body is not all of you, and to know that divinity exists within— these are insights that will set you free to pursue the vision through which your divinity can flower. This is perfect enlightenment and a complete life. This is salvation. This is a blessing.

There Is No Beginning and No End

The word information is very familiar. It has become more familiar ever since computers became such a large part of our lives. Although the first image that comes to mind now when someone says "information" is the computer, when I was a child, information was something that was passed along in secret from a spy to an agent in hushed whispers or in notes wrapped inside newspapers.

Today information is a part of everyday life, and our lives have been organized around it. The meaning of information has expanded to include not only writing and symbols, but music and pictures. Everything has been "datafied" and "informationalized." Living in this sea of information, have you ever asked yourself what information is and how it exists?

Information Is Zero

The definition of information has shifted throughout the ages as technology has advanced. In ancient Mesopotamia, information was symbols on pressed clay; in Egypt, information was figures drawn on papyrus paper; in China, information was the irregular patterns on the back of a turtle's shell. After the invention of the printing press, information was printed writing in books. Now, with the widespread use of computers, information is no longer limited to the realm of paper, pencil, or pen.

In twenty-first-century parlance, information is a magnetic pattern left by an electric current as it flows over a medium, such as a computer disk. The term "software" that we use so often these days refers not to the CDs or disks, but to the information they contain. How will the definition of information expand in the future with further advances in technology? Information could mean a flow of wind, or even the distribution of cells inside the brain. However, no matter how the definition expands or changes, it still refers to the method employed to record information; it doesn't tell you what information actually is.

The reason that we need a material medium, such as paper, pencil, and disks, to process information is a testament to the limitations of technology, not to the essential nature of information itself. For example, the ideas in themselves recorded on a disk or on a 5,000-year-old reed tablet are not tangible or visible and do not occupy space or time. These ideas left traces in these human-made recording devices, tools used to fix ideas in a three-dimensional mode. However, what about the original idea represented? Does it still exist? If so, in what form? Information, although it surely exists, does not take up any position in time or space. This is an essential aspect of information.

In mathematical terms, information occupies the position of zero. When you add zero to zero, it's still zero. When you multiply zero with zero, it's also zero. It is a zero, it can be duplicated infinitely. A million zeroes are the same as the original zero. We experience this aspect of information in computer networking. One piece of information in a form of a picture can appear in one or in one hundred computer monitors at the same time. On the Internet, tens of thousand of users can access the same information simultaneously. Information exists independently of output frequency. This is the essential nature of information and of zero. Information is zero.

Nothingness and Emptiness

Compare an image projected onto a screen three feet away and a screen thirty feet away. Which image will be larger? Of course, the image on a screen thirty feet away would be far larger. Assuming that the projector is powerful enough, then the image on a screen 300 feet away would be even larger. However, no matter how large the image gets, the information contained by this image is the same throughout, zero. Zero, because the image is just a reflection or the expression of the information that lies behind its reality. The image is not the information itself.

A three-foot projection of Mt. Everest and a life-sized projection of Mt. Everest are different in terms of size, but not in terms of information. Information itself is not bound by the space and time within which the projected image exists. This is the realm of information, which, although it exists, does not occupy time nor space.

You could look into every tiny corner of this large projected image, but you would not find the information reality behind it. No matter how far you travel, or how deep you delve, you are still within the confines of the projected image. You cannot capture that "something" behind the image.

This reminds me of Mandelbrot's images. A brilliant mathematician, Benoit Mandelbrot is the father of fractal geometry, and his equation is often used in chaos theory. The special characteristic of Mandelbrot's design is that, on the surface, it looks extremely intricate and complicated. However, these constantly varying and intricate images are created by a simple set of equations. Any section of the image, when magnified, is identical to the image as a whole. This happens no matter how much you increase the magnification.

You will never find the set of equations behind the image, no matter how long or how deeply you examine the image. Only when you have the insight to discern the underlying order behind such complicated imagery will you get a glimpse of the equation that drives the image. What is this equation if not information, occupying neither space nor time? This information, a zero by definition, is the driving creative force behind an intricate and magnificent image. Zero, therefore, contains infinite possibilities and an infinite range of expression. The imagery may belong in the world of output and expression, but the equation that provides it belongs in the realm of information.

In a futile effort to find the underlying truth of existence, we peer into the farthest reaches of the universe and split subatomic particles into smaller units. However, these techniques will only enable us to see the smallest particles that the prevailing technology affords. It will not help us "see" the reality behind existence, which is information. Since the world of information is zero, even the tiniest particle is larger than zero. Zero cannot be captured by the most sensitive radar nor the most powerful electron microscope. Why? Because it's zero. How can you see that which is nothing?

You can describe the world of zero as nothingness or emptiness. Mathematically, zero is nothing, and, in physics, zero is termed empty. Information can be described as the pattern of waves upon this "body of water" called zero. But how would you differentiate between waves and water? This is why I call the realm of information the realm of zero. You cannot separate the water from the waves. How then could we recognize this realm of 0? There is only one radar in the world sensitive enough to detect this world, and that is your mind. If you truly want to know the source of existence, look deeply into your own mind first.

Look around you. You see many objects: the clock on the wall, the cup on the table. Without any thought, observe these objects. How do you know that they are actually there? What if these objects are just images projected onto a screen called three-dimensional reality? What is the reality behind these images? This is nothingness and emptiness.

The existence of every "something" is based on a "nothing." The realm of nothingness and emptiness is the root of all existences. This realm cannot be reached by getting on a spaceship and traveling to the ends of the known universe. This realm is not at the far edges of existence, but inside all existence. Therefore, zero is not merely nothingness, but the source and background of all expressions of existence. Your thoughts are wave patterns on the surface of the sea of zero, and the objects that you see are the resulting output of that pattern.

If zero is the ocean, and information is the pattern of waves that sweeps across the surface of the water, what then is the wind that creates these waves? I call this the Life Current. Just as an electric current moves over a medium to encase information within a magnetic pattern, the Life Current moves through the realm of zero to create patterns. In a word, it creates information. When you participate in this process, you call it imagination—having a thought or idea, or feelings.

The Three Basic Processes of All Existence

We can now grasp the three basic processes of existence. One, at the source and background of all existence lies the sea of nothingness. Two, a current of life force draws an infinite array of patterns upon this sea. Three, material ingredients are used to express these patterns.

When Life Current flows over the sea of nothingness to create a pattern that is expressed using the material ingredients, we call the result the world. These three processes act in harmony to create all existence. Most often, these three processes are called *Chun-Ji-In* in ancient Oriental teachings. *Chun* refers to Heaven, *Ji* to Earth, and *In* to the Human. Although these concepts transcend time and space, if we had to arrange them, Heaven would come first, then Earth, with the Human moving in between the two.

Heaven is analogous to the realm of nothingness, Earth to the material ingredients needed to give expression to a pattern, which is created by the Life Current, or Human. Of course, the term Heaven, as it is used here, does not refer to the blue sky above us, Earth to the soil under your feet, or Human to you or me. I use these terms to facilitate an intellectual understanding of cosmic truth.

The Life Current is the main actor in creation, and the omnipresent divine reality in existence. Life Current, in physical terms, is a particle without mass or size, and in functional terms, it is a particle that carries thought. Since it doesn't have mass, it doesn't have gravity, and since it is without mass, it is not trapped within space; this allows it to travel from the realm of zero to the infinitely variable world of material output, and back.

When we are able to feel this flow of Life Current, we name it Ki. Through this current, much information is created, information that acts as a blueprint that directs the flow of energy that acts on matter to bring an image into a three-dimensional reality, into a world of shapes and forms. These images come together to fill the world we live in.

The realm of nothingness over which the Life Current flows is a world of no preconditions. It is a world of absolute freedom and true creation. Nothingness or emptiness cannot be recognized or perceived as such. Just as we hang a "Caution" sign on a transparent glass door, we have to etch a pattern on this nothingness in order to perceive its existence. It is through the etched pattern that we not only recognize the pattern but realize the existence of the glass. Imagine a pool of transparent water, still as a vacuum, without activity. Then a breeze blows across it and causes ripples to move across its surface. Only then can we feel the coolness of the wind and discern the existence of the pool of water.

Therefore, when a Life Current passes over the surface of the sea of nothingness and creates a pattern of waves, it not only creates an informational pattern that is used to build the world of shapes and forms but it alerts us to the existence of the sea itself. Therefore, through the flow of Life Current, nothingness is revealed, somethingness is produced, and nothingness is recognized as the source of all somethingness. This is the grand harmony, a ceaseless cosmic motion. This wind of life upon the sea of nothingness is sometimes termed *Yuln'yo* in the Korean spiritual traditions.

Among these endless cycles of movements and patterns, some of which are expressed in material shapes and forms, can anything be singled out as the truth? Truth, in actuality, is the whole process by which nothingness and somethingness are revealed by the flow of the Life Current, differentiated but connected. The process itself is the truth, not separate, observable steps within the process. The movements of the Life Current leave a residue on our minds, and out of those residues that our minds can recognize, we convert an even smaller fraction of that into words and languages in a process of simplification.

Therefore, a truth that has been intellectually digested and expressed through words can only be a shadow of the silhouette of the original truth. It is but the most minute traces of the truth. This applies even to the words I am writing now, to all the sacred texts ever written, and to the sayings of all the great enlightened teachers in the history of humankind. If you could bring together all the words ever generated in an attempt to explain the truth, it would be no more momentous than a yawn. This is the stark limitation of language.

The truth is the movement, the process occurring right at this moment. Therefore, although you can become one with the truth, you cannot intellectually recognize or explain it. To see and recognize the truth, you have to separate yourself from the truth. To explain the truth in words, you have to separate yourself from the recognition. This is why a truth that has been wordsmithed is only a shadow of the barest silhouette of the truth. A yawn would contain more truth than that.

Creation, Evolution, and Editing

Life Current, the protagonist in the drama of the truth, resides in all forms of existence. This can also be referred as the divine ubiquitous in all existence. However, depending upon its frequency and range of use, the form, shape, and method of its residence differs markedly. The higher its degree of activity, the higher its vibrational frequency, the wider its range of activity and the greater its powers of creation. When the activity of a Life Current is below a certain level, we consider it lifeless. Even among a single living system, the brightness of its activity and frequency of its vibration depends upon the rate of its use, determining the level of the consciousness in which it resides.

The level of brightness of the Life Current can, in the human case, be organized in a spectrum that reflects the pattern of thoughts and behaviors exhibited by individuals. In terms of energy, the differences in brightness can be described as a matter of differences in energy expenditure. However, in human terms, since energy is expressed through filters called emotions and thoughts, the individual awareness or brightness levels have to be determined by observing the patterns in one's thoughts and behaviors.

When a person's awareness has attained a consistent level of brightness, only then is he able to see himself. This is a physical fact. Imagine lighting an oil lamp in a dark room. As the lamp wick starts to burn, the light gradually gets brighter. Gradually, with the ever-brightening light, you are able to see your hands, arms, and, eventually, your whole body. When you can see yourself, you become self-conscious and act with more care. When the light becomes bright enough for you to start discerning others in the room, you start acting with decorum, becoming considerate of others. And because you can now see yourself, you start asking why you are here. Only then have you taken your first step towards going back home. As the flow of Life Current becomes stronger within you, your awareness becomes brighter, giving you more insight and knowledge. When the activity level of your Life Current reaches a certain point of critical mass, it changes into a different and advanced form, much like a butterfly climbing out of a cocoon. This is the meaning of evolution.

The process of evolution whereby a life form activates and strengthens its own life energy begins with the birth of its soul. The birth of the soul means that the Life Current coalesces around a single nucleus. We refer to this entity as the soul. The nucleus of a soul is that one thought that does not dissipate or dissolve even with time. Usually, this nucleus is a strong desire or an unquench-able hope. This thought becomes the seed around which the Life Current gathers to form one consistent unit. As long as this seed remains viable—in other words, until the hope or desire becomes fulfilled—the soul will maintain a consistent identity.

We can make an analogy to a lake fed by a stream and which empties into another stream below. The flow of the water remains unimpeded, constantly replenishing the water in the lake, and the shape of the lake remains consistent. Likewise, although the Life Current is always flowing, the soul keeps its shape, as does the lake.

While keeping its shape constant, the soul begins a journey to satisfy the desire or hope that forms its nucleus. By satisfy, we mean either achieve or "output" the shape or form envisioned by the hope. If the soul somehow manages to succeed in a single try, then the hope is quenched and the nucleus dissolved, allowing the Life Current to go back to its original state. The lake goes back to being just water. However, if it doesn't succeed at its first attempt, it repeats the attempt again and again, adding new ideas and edit-ing the old. It's akin to you creating a picture or a document in your computer.

The process that we call creation is therefore a conscious action whereby information is generated, outputted, experienced, and then upgraded or deleted according to the results of the experi-ence. It is an "editing" process. Rewriting the sentence, shortening or lengthening the paragraph, resizing the picture, changing the background color—in this vein, the term karma refers to the mounds of information stored in layers during the repeated attempts at "editing."

The repeated output of existing but imperfect information is called *Samsara* in Buddhist lingo, or reincarnation, or transmi-gration of the soul. Karma not only refers to the process whereby genetic information in DNA creates the proteins that make up our physical bodies, but also to the overall life condition in which our physical bodies reside. Energy follows the pattern laid out by this informational blueprint of karma, organizing the material ingredients into specific shapes and forms, including our bodies and our living conditions.

Three Truths and Three Falsehoods

During this process of outputting, editing, and re-outputting, new information is added in layers until the original nucleus of the soul may become overshadowed. I am sure you have experienced something similar many times. After repeated editing, you lose sight of the original idea that you were trying to produce in the first place. You forget what the drawing was originally supposed to look like. As these shells of information pile up higher and higher, you run the risk of having this information pile act as master of the house.

Referring to this information pile, we can use the terms false self or ego. We can also use the term personality or character. When this pile of information tries to act as the owner, it is the same as a house guest pretending to be the master of the house while the real master is asleep in the upstairs bedroom. Since the soul has been effectively covered over and has forgotten its original purpose, the information that you generated becomes your substitute goal, the object of your pursuit. You thereby add karma to your already existing karma.

When you see the truth through this prism of self-generated shells of information, you don't see it unadulterated. You don't see the continuity, only the disparate components, like a ray of light broken up through a prism. You don't see the nothingness, but only the patterns etched onto its surface; you don't see the Life Current, but only the trace feeling of its flow. You don't see the matter, but only the already constructed products. Because of the grand illusion called separateness, you don't recognize the whole but only see a part under close-up inspection. We often call such recognition phenomena the mind.

Say you were typing a document on your computer when someone turned off the power switch and the document you were working on disappeared without being saved. Something disappeared, but what? The power cord is still plugged in, the program is still on the hard drive, and the hardware is as solid as ever. What disappeared? In fact, nothing. Everything is as it was before. The only thing that disappeared is the phenomenon created in a collaboration of hardware, software, and electricity. The thing disappeared is the surface phenomenon created by the workings of these three factors.

However, the basic three factors that created the phenomenon in the first place are still extant and active. Your mind is the phenomenon, as are the words in the document. In other words, the mind is not a stand-alone, quantifiable phenomenon, but an expression of the workings of the energy and the soul that have come together temporarily in this physical manifestation called the body. Therefore, "mind" is just a reflection created by the body's brain manipulated by the deeper reality of the soul and energy.

The nothingness that is the reality of your mind is forever and unchanging. However, the surface patterns on this sea of nothingness, our emotions and thoughts, are in constant flux. We grasp at one particular segment of a pattern among countless other patterns and declare it to be "mine." These "mine" patterns gather to weave an identity called "me." Try to dissect this "me." "Me" is just a collection of "mines." We would shed blood and tears to protect and secure what is ultimately merely information, because we think that these patterns are reality.

When you first set out on a trip, you do so with the thought of returning. However, once you embark on a trip, you can never guarantee your return date. If you knew this, would you still be able to call birth a blessing? In fact, the best you can do in life is to return home. This is the break-even point. But since you are born, you have to work hard to return home because you want to cut the difficult journey as short as possible. Just in case you have forgotten your way back home or have lost sight of your destination, you need a guide, meditation technique, or spiritual training to help you remember.

Journey Starts with a Single Thought

Every trip begins with a single thought, hope, or desire. Where did this thought, the nucleus of the soul, come from? Whose thought is it anyway? Who should take responsibility for this thought? Isn't it unfair, looking from the soul's point of view, to have to take a long and arduous journey because of a thought that it had no part in creating?

If you look at this issue through the prism of your information pile, you might think it unfair. However, the soul will gladly undertake this journey as its responsibility and do its utmost to help the seed bloom, for a soul is purity itself, with no judgments or discrimination. The pure soul knows that this seed is the responsibility of the whole of existence. Have you ever seen a dandelion? When the plant is mature, it awaits the coming of a breeze to carry the seed away. The seed sprouts into another dandelion plant. The dandelion has just engaged in a process of realizing the information contained within its seed. The dandelion did not choose to be born as a dandelion; however, the dandelion would not complain about its existence, even if it could. The best you can do with your life, once you have taken a physical form, is to live to the best of your abilities and nurture the seed of hope that forms the nucleus of your soul.

How long does a soul have to undertake this journey? The length of the journey depends upon how quickly you achieve that one thought, desire, or hope that forms the soul's nucleus. Some hopes are quickly realized while others take longer. Some hopes are simple enough to be realized quickly while others need more time. Some hopes need to wait for a propitious moment to bloom.

Go out to a field of flowers. Some are small, some are large, some are colorful, some are strikingly simple. Some wither quickly and some stay in bloom for a long time. The shapes and sizes of the flowers all differ, even among the same types. Which flower do you like? What color do you prefer? You can pick the flower that your taste prefers, but there is no good or bad.

A large flower just happens to be large while a small flower is just small. A long-lasting flower lasts long while others wither more quickly. There is a great diversity, but there is neither superiority nor inferiority. Although each flower is beautiful in its own fashion, there is a greater and more magnificent beauty in the whole of this picture, with flowers withering, blooming, sprouting, decaying, petals fluttering in the wind, such that the whole is much more beautiful than the parts. This is the Garden of God.

Within this magnificent garden, countless seeds are scattered and countless flowers bloom. Even now, you are scattering countless seeds of hopes and thoughts into a field of nothingness plowed and fertilized by the Life Current. The seeds of hopes you scatter into the field are even now taking root and causing the births of innumerable souls, actions, and lives. Just as you are living the life you have been given, they will live the lives that they have been given. Some will scatter in the wind while others will live out several lifetimes before finding their way back.

A seed, once planted, has the right to sprout, whether it be bad or good. You can choose whether to plant or not, or which seed to plant, but you have no right to gainsay a seed's right to grow once it's planted. A seed, once planted, will never just fade away. The seed will bring forth a life from which more seeds will arise. Thus the cycle continues endlessly.

There is no hidden meaning or intent in this cycle. It just goes on, continuously. It just is. There is, in fact, no meaning to life. Because this truth is too empty to bear, we look for even a grain of meaning and expand upon it and build it up until we become prisoners of the "meaning cage" of our own construction. We construct an artificial justification for our lives when life needs no justification. And while living thus forgetfully, we encounter an event that compels us to finish what we came to do and to go back to where we came from in the first place.

Enlightenment Is Not the End but the Beginning

The journey consists of a single seed of thought, which flowers and withers, returning to its original place. People often call the end of this journey "enlightenment." What does enlightenment mean? What do you have to know to be enlightened? Is enlightenment the end? What could be behind enlightenment?

The crux of enlightenment is that there is nothing to be enlightened about. When you realize that there is nothing to be enlightened about, that is enlightenment. Does it sound funny? Fishy? Let us think for a moment. The conscious mind that so desires enlightenment is merely a temporary phenomenon without underlying reality. The real mind, which is the sea of nothingness from which all existence springs, has never not known something. To summarize, the mind that desires enlightenment is actually without reality, while the real mind is the definition of enlightenment itself. Who is it that wants to be enlightened, and to what? There is no enlightenment, and efforts to achieve enlightenment are by definition futile—this is true enlightenment.

Therefore, enlightenment is a new start for the journey, not the end. Until now, we wandered aimlessly through many lifetimes and went through untold experiences because we did not know how or why this journey started. But now we remember the original purpose of the journey, and this helps us find our way to the destination. This is the reason we need enlightenment. Have you ever gone out on an errand on a warm spring day and been led astray by the trembling beauty of a butterfly, forgetting the purpose of your errand? Your mother probably told you numerous times to go straight to the store and come back, a warning you promptly forgot. Your mother knew that although you would eventually return home, for there was nowhere else to go, the time of your return was open-ended.

This is why enlightenment is the beginning of a new journey. Chasing the butterfly, you suddenly remember, "Oh yes, I was on my way to the market to buy flour" or: "I was on my way to a neighbor's house to borrow a hammer." This is enlightenment. So, you leave the butterfly behind (with some wistfulness) and continue with your original errand. This is where the teacher comes in. A teacher is someone who reminds you of the errand. However, the teacher does not run the errand for you. You have to go yourself, borrow the tool or buy the flour, and return home safely, without getting sidetracked. Only then will this journey end, and will your soul end its time as this particular incarnation.

The lake will then become just water again. The nucleus that held the soul together need no longer be maintained, for it has been satisfied. Therefore, the Life Current that coalesced around this nucleus is loosed from the chain that bound it to the soul. Once free, it goes back to its original condition of absolute freedom.

No one knows how long this freedom will last. The time of freedom, from another point of view, could be the time before the Life Current is called forth again to come together around another seed of hope and give shape to another soul about to embark on a new journey. It is getting ready to dream a new dream. Just as our bodies decay and provide material for new life, Life Current is recycled continuously to serve the needs of the soul. This process is happening naturally without waiting for someone to attach a label or meaning to it. Put in human terms, we could call it an act of sacrifice and highest love, for it willingly gives up absolute freedom to help one seed of hope to come to fruition and be realized.

The Meaning of Karma

How does your life look? How can you live "right?" What life do you choose? You have already traveled far. Regardless of whether you want it or not, all the actions you took and the experiences you underwent are with you as a karmic record, influencing what you do now. However, the important thing is when you seek to choose your life, your power of choice also has the ability to cut off any lingering karmic connections. Of course, this does not mean that the information which is karma just disappears. Like it or not, karmic debt is a real debt you must pay, now or later. However, now you no longer will be led around helplessly by your karma but you can gain insight to use this information to achieve your ends.

By mentioning karma here, I don't intend to talk about reincarnation or previous lives. Even if a previous life exists and can be recalled, it has no reality other than as a piece of information expressed in this current lifetime. When you buy a computer, it comes with an operating system installed. This is akin to karma. The operating system is karma. The computer is karma.

Some people buy a computer with Windows 98; some buy it with the latest XP version; others are saddled with an older version such as 3.1 or DOS. Some computers also run with the latest processor chip while some still run an XX286 chip. Just as Windows is already set up in your hardware and your computer is equipped with a processor chip, so is your karma expressed in your physical form and living conditions as soon as you are born. Except here there is no good or bad, or superior or inferior models, for information is essentially all zero. How can one zero be better than another? Your previous lifetimes can be compared to a period in which you installed "programs" and prepared your "computer" to do the work that you need to do in this lifetime. It doesn't matter whether you recall your previous lifetime or not. It is just information, after all. In fact, instead of saying "record of my life," it would be more accurate to say "record of a life as recorded in my brain." Nothing matters except the realization that you are living in the here and now with various piles of information. Only this life is your life, not your previous life or your future incarnations.

When I expound on karma, I do so not to dwell on the mysticism generated by the term but merely wish to emphasize the importance of choice and responsibility. When Buddha taught about karma, he did so to teach his students about choices and responsibilities, not to mystify life and give it justification. Likewise, when Jesus said that you would gain the doors of heaven when you repent, he wanted to lift self-condemning people out from under the weight of guilt, not to give a green light to wanton and remorseless sins. Buddha and Jesus taught the universal truth the way they did, not because their way was the only way, but because they considered their ways appropriate to solve the spiritual problems of their times.

Say you headed East for a long time and have come far. Your trip, your steps so far, are recorded in your brain and reflected in the actual position in which you are standing now. This is a fact and has nothing to do with whether you believe in karma or not. The more important thing is where do you go from here? Is there a reason for you to walk in the same direction as you have? Yes, if you know that this is the direction in which your hope lies. However, if you walk in the same direction for no particular reason, then you are subjecting yourself to carelessness and continuing habit, which have nothing to do with your karma. You always can choose your direction.

Ask Your Heart and Talk with Your Brain

If your choice requires you to completely change your life, change directions, and leave the comfort and security of the path that you have walked so far, it is natural for hesitation and second thoughts to accompany such a decision. However, as you know already, more calculations and deliberation do not make the choice any easier or wiser. Ultimately, the decision is a one-time choice.

The question to ask is simple: What is it you really want? What are the things that fill your heart with hope and joy? Ask your soul and heart this question. There is no guarantee that your choice is the one that corresponds to that original hope that acted as the seed around which your soul was built. However, if you don't ask your soul, where else would you direct the question? If not to your heart, then where?

The soul is pure. Since it is pure, it is simple. It knows what it wants and it is always ready to do anything to get it. Once you have asked your soul and received the answer through your heart, then it is time to discuss how to go about getting it with your brain. Your brain is a monitor that displays the movement of the Life Current and records its paths. Your brain is part of your basic equipment to help you on your journey, much like a notebook computer you take on business trips.

Unfortunately, in many cases, the brain is infected with a "virus" that renders its main program inoperable. Now it is time to reorganize the files and reactivate the main program by finding and deleting that virus. Throw away the files you don't need and reorganize the ones you do. Then you will realize how good the equipment that you have on your journey is. Remember, you have to do hardware and software maintenance to keep your computer running at optimum efficiency. Hardware maintenance consists of allowing your brain to breathe and relax properly, while software maintenance is feeding constructive and "good" information into your brain.

How easily you will travel and how far you will go depends on how well you use your brain. If you use your brain well, it will make your journey much easier. If you don't organize the information in your brain, you will encounter hardship and misdirection, adding misery to your trip. Whatever the case, you have to finish the race by running the distance allotted to you. When your soul reaches the destination and achieves what it originally sought to achieve, only then is it freed from its responsibility and allowed to return to its original nothingness state of zero. This is the salvation of the soul, to have come back to where it started. This is why there is no beginning and no end.

Conclusion: The Meaning of Living Right

We started by talking about computers, and we have come a long way since that. We need a concrete conclusion that can help us live this life. Knowing what we know now, what is meant by "living right"? If we see only the patterns and not the reality behind them, we will always live in anxiety and fear, although it might be punctuated by fleeting moments of gaiety. If we see only the nothingness and not the marvelous pictures created by the flow of Life Current, we will sink into a morass of inactivity and emptiness.

Some people mistakenly think emptiness itself is enlightenment. This is definitely not so. It's like going into a theater after the movie is over and staring at the empty screen. Seeing the world correctly means you perceive the harmonious process of *Chun-Ji-In* while enjoying the sights of its creations at the same time.

I would define a "right" attitude toward life thus: Do not worry or fear, for you will always have a home to go back to, which is the eternal, all-encompassing sea of nothingness. Do not feel empty or bored, for you will always encounter the indescribable beauty of life. Burying the root of existence deep in the field of nothingness, live forever now with a bright vision in your heart.

Does this sound like the familiar saying "Do your best with what you have"? Well, in a way it is. It might disappoint you that the highest insight you will get after all this is *carpe diem,* which means "seize the day." But what can I say? I want to help you, and this is the quickest and only way to achieve your goal. No matter what manner of wisdom you have attained, there is no other way to live right other than to live honestly, diligently, and responsibly. Such fair transactions comprise the nucleus of the truth and the essence of Tao as I know it.

Sharing My Story: Why Do I Do What I Do?

Finally, I would like to share an insight from my own story. Like yours, this journey of mine has not been easy. I have come through all the aforementioned steps and am still traveling on my journey to take responsibility for my choices. Countless souls have taken this path, and countless more souls will in one way or another follow the same path. This is a journey in which the best you can do is to break even. However, no one can stop the journey.

Even now, innumerable souls are being born out of the seeds of limitless ideas, dreams, and hopes. Although I cannot stop this journey, I would like to set up better signs, information booths, and rest areas to help the travelers on the way. I want to do this because this trip has been so difficult for me. If you have ever climbed a mountain on a harsh and unfamiliar trail and found some measure of unexpected comfort from a piece of ribbon or a pile of marking stones left behind by a previous climber, then you will know how I feel. To help people cut short their spiritual wanderings, to help them discover the divinity within, to help this divinity flower, to help them go back sooner to where they will eventually go, to create favorable conditions for the perfection of the soul—this is what I choose to do.

If birth itself is not a blessing, what about birth into an atmosphere in which it is impossible to complete the purpose of your birth? If this is not an outright curse, it is close to it. From your point of view, what about our Earth today? What would be the impression of a soul who opens its eyes on Earth? Let us say that you are having a baby. Giving birth is, like it or not, inviting a soul to come to Earth to embark on a journey for its perfection. Is Earth an appropriate place to which to invite a soul to complete its divine journey? Do you think that Earth today is a good place to promote the growth of a soul?

Even God's "house" has a garbage can. The most negative information in the world is still information, and, as such, has the right and hope to become realized. Divine garbage, or Hell, is a place that has the conditions in which negative information can most readily attain reality. When good information gathers, it creates the conditions under which it can prosper by expressing itself in reality. When bad information gathers, it also creates the conditions under which it can be realized.

We, as humanity, stand at the edge of this narrow ledge. Whether Earth will be a good training ground for helping souls to reach perfection or whether it will become the universal ghetto of negative information is our choice.

I want to make the current conditions on Earth better than they are now. I want to make Earth an ideal place for spiritual growth, a cosmic showcase such that souls will line up and take numbers to get in. I have chosen to give my all and sacrifice everything I have to achieve this goal. I have so far remained true to my choice. This is the healing that I speak of. For me, healing society and healing Earth are my ways of actualizing my enlightenment and being responsible for my choices.

I don't consider this my individual work. I believe there are many souls on Earth whose goal is to engage in similar work. The reason I am sharing my story is that I think you are one of those souls.

God's Sudden-Death Game

When Europeans first came to America, they made the land theirs in a variety of ways. At first, they were given land, then they bought the land, and finally, they forcibly seized the land. When they first bought the land, they bought it at a price far below the land's potential for production. When they first signed the contract to the land, they probably looked at the Native Americans who were selling the land and said, "Pity the fools. How foolish to sell this much land for such a low price."

The Native Americans probably thought, "Pity the fools, to pay good money for land, which you can't even carry on horseback, when you can just go and live on it." Trouble came when different concepts and expectations of these two people clashed. Europeans did not think that the Native Americans would freely use the land even after they sold it, and the Native Americans could not imagine that the Europeans would post a fence around the land and prevent others from trespassing. Which were the fools? How did we ever come across the idea that land could be owned, that humanity owned the Earth?

The Human Road

Let us assume that Earth is about five billion years old and the first ancestors to modern-day *Homo sapiens* emerged from the primordial swamp (so to speak) about three million years ago. Even extending the average human life span to a generous 100 years old, three million years is a long time. No wonder we think that Earth is ours, since we have been here so long. However, compared to the five-billion-year history of Earth, our three million is not so impressive, especially considering that it was only 50,000 years ago or so that we started using tools and exhibiting possibilities for becoming the dominant species on Earth that we are now.

Or are we now? There are two facts cited when humans are claimed to be the dominant species. One, we monopolize the highest percentage of Earth's natural resources. Two, we are the most threatening species, capable of annihilating other species and destroying the Earth. Therefore, humans are the dominant species on Earth in much the same way as the biggest bully on the block gets that way due to his size. We might argue that humans are different or special because of our intellectual pursuits and cultural achievements, but truthfully, do you think that Earth would be less beautiful or harmonious without Mozart's symphonies or Shakespeare's sonnets?

If we were to recognize the right of first claim to the land, then Earth would belong to the ants and cockroaches before it did to us. Since they lived here longer than we have, instead of spraying insecticides whenever we spot them, we should be paying them rent. Dinosaurs, which disappeared abruptly from the face of the Earth about sixty-five million years ago, were the dominant species on Earth for 150 million years. Compared to their reign, the human reign hasn't even started yet.

As human beings strengthened their claim to the top spot, our relationship to Earth became ever more fragile and anxiety-ridden. In an ever-increasing attempt to secure our living conditions, we utilized non-sustainable and non-justifiable (except for greed) methods of mining the environment, methods which have led to scarcity and barrenness. As a result, we have come to this point at which we not only threaten Earth but also our own survival. If we don't overcome the challenge of survival facing us, we will have existed only for about 50,000 years as a recognizable species, which, compared to the estimated five billion years of Earth's life span, is not even as long as the blink of an eye.

Although natural evolution is a field still marked by unanswered and unanswerable questions, two questions are generally thought to be foremost in the field: What caused the quick demise of the dinosaurs, and what caused the meteoric rise of *Homo sapiens* as the dominant presence on Earth?

Although scientists have found fossilized bones of our presumed ancestors dating back some three million years, it is still subject to debate whether we descended from these ancestors. We have yet to find the missing link. All we know for sure is that *Homo sapiens,* after maintaining a quiet presence for most of the three million years, began a rapid upwards climb about 50,000 years ago, showing amazing intellectual and creative progress with the beginning of the Neolithic Age 15,000 years ago. It was almost as if human beings made a great leap forward—no, a gigantic leap forward—in terms of intellectual abilities.

Why did the dinosaurs suddenly disappear and human beings emerge, among all the species, as masters of an intellect that has since advanced enough to now threaten the entire Earth? Although scientific inquiry will take some time to complete, if it ever is completed, I have done some creative thinking of my own and drafted a plausible scenario to answer these questions. Bear with me as we embark on a fun journey of "what-if?"

Project Omega: A Harmonious Life Community

Once, a very long time ago, about fifty billion years ago, the gods embarked on a new and important project. Advanced life forms from all across the universe (gods), gathered to discuss whether it was possible for a community of varying life forms to live in harmony; that is, to develop a peaceful universal community. Thus a new project was born.

They created a planet called the Earth, and provided it with favorable conditions for life, equipping it with a Sun in the most fashionable neighborhood of the universe. They were careful to provide every possible life amenity and didn't leave out any detail. Since they were gods, you can imagine how thorough they must have been. Then they copied parts of their own genetic information and gave birth to new life forms made in their image.

However, knowing that the genetic traits of divinity or creativity were potentially dangerous in immature hands, they left these areas undeveloped until they deemed that the life forms had reached an evolutionary stage capable of dealing with such powers. They watched the life forms further diversify themselves into different species and watched the path of evolution that each species followed. They watched how the species interacted with one another, for that was the crux of their experiment. Since the original intent was to see if different life forms could develop a harmonious relationship among themselves, it was decided that gods would not interfere in this process.

Turn Divinity on or Not?

The project went on until an unforeseen situation compelled the gods to interfere: the explosive growth of the dinosaurs. At the top of the food chain, the dinosaurs not only had an insatiable appetite but also a fierce character that harmed every species of the sea, air, and land. The dinosaurs eventually reached a point beyond which they would have threatened the survival of other species on Earth. So the gods discussed the problem and voted unanimously to rid the Earth of the dinosaurs. Therefore, they loosed a virus that selectively destroyed only the dinosaurs, and then they were no more.

After this incident, the life forms on Earth went on their evolutionary way again. Some became extinct and some prospered, but none presented a threat to the whole. When the life forms reached a certain evolutionary stage, gods decided it was time to unlock the powers of creativity. The human was the most ideal candidate, for it had developed bipedalism, a trait that was conducive to the expression of creativity, through an evolutionary accident. Another consideration in humanity's favor was that the human was a relatively shy and unassuming creature, who, even with the powers of divine creativity, would not pose a threat to other species on Earth. In contrast, imagine a lion with a human's powers of intellect.

A grand controversy ensued. One side argued that following the original intent of the experiment, they had to unlock the divine creative potential in humans to see if one created could develop into a creator and establish a peaceful and harmonious community among diverse life forms. The other side argued that such a power, once unleashed, would tempt the humans to lord it over other species and eventually to destroy themselves and the Earth because their intellectual capacities would not be able to deal with their divine creativity.

Those that favored unlocking the divine creative potential wore white robes and the opposition wore black. This division represented a more fundamental division among the gods: one side wanted to expand the use of the divine creativity in all areas of the universe and, accordingly, went around planting seeds of divine information. The other side wanted to limit the use of divine creativity, and was consequently busy scooping up the seeds of divine information that the white-robed ones had scattered.

However, knowing that they represented opposite but necessary sides that brought a balanced tension to the universe, each side respected the work of the other. But in the case of the Omega Experiment, as we might call this project, they needed unanimity among the gods in order to take any action, since it was originally conceived and begun as a collective project. Therefore, the debate intensified.

The Decision: Humans Will Have Divine Creativity

At the height of the debate, the white-robed gods suggested a radical idea: if the gods followed their suggestion and the project failed, then they would change into black robes, signifying a fundamental change in the direction of the universe. This is logical, for even gods have to take responsibilities for their choices. Choice is free, but one must take responsibility for its consequences. This is the rule that a creator has to follow. The black-robed gods agreed to this arrangement and the project proceeded with a unanimous vote to unlock the divine creative potential in humans.

The gods used a form of virus which, when embedded in human cells, unlocks and activates genes for divine creativity. The effect was immediate and enormous, for human brains expanded, surprising even the gods who had initiated the action with the speed of its progress. The white-robed gods gave the gift of hope and joy to humans as tools to use its newly-found powers, while the black-robed gods planted guilt and shame to discourage the use of these powers.

The divine creative power was designed to have two modes of expression. One was the "enlightenment" mode and the other was the "creative" mode. These two capabilities were designed to develop in conjunction with each other, so that humans would gain an insight into the question "Who am I?" as they exercised the creative powers of a creator. However, the synchronization did not materialize as expected, and the creative mode developed far faster and farther than the enlightenment mode, leaving humans to engage in unconscious and irresponsible creation.

Humans, not realizing the divinity within them, became drunk on their own superficial creative powers and thought themselves absolute masters of Earth. Humans monopolized Earth's resources and threatened the very survival of the species with which the gods had populated the Earth, thinking it their inherent right as humans. This resulted in a flood of S.O.S.s from the life forms suffering under the human tyranny on Earth.

Meanwhile, the original supporters for unlocking the divine creative potential in humans, the white-robed gods, sometimes made an appearance on Earth in various disguises to inject the human psyche with good and positive information and to clean up the bad and negative information. During their time on Earth, these gods, within the limitations imposed by their human manifestations, strove to wake up the enlightenment mode of humans.

In the beginning, many high gods visited Earth with this purpose; the traces of their visits are recorded in legends and myths. Some of these gods mated with humans and left descendants with whom they created model communities of cooperation and harmony for all humans to follow, hoping that such a coexistence model would become the norm on Earth. Many other gods came after them, and their stories have come down to us in more concrete forms. Although each had his style, all had one common theme: Activate the enlightenment mode embedded in the human psyche. Instead of following the gods' teachings faithfully, however, humans twisted and idolized the teachings, turning them into religions. Although a few humans managed to reach the cusp of enlightenment, the majority remained at a very low level of conscious awareness.

Crisis: To Go or Stop?

Then an incident occurred that prompted the gods to call an emergency meeting: the humans invented the nuclear bomb. They had actually used the bomb to annihilate a portion of their own number! Like a foolish child who sets his own house on fire by playing with matches and is now looking at the burning house from the inside with amazement and joy, humans who had unleashed the destructive power of the atom were smug and self-satisfied, daring others to challenge their suddenly paramount power lest they, too, be destroyed.

The natural outcome of such a situation was that human groups would also make nuclear bombs and engage in a destructive competition of weapons of mass destruction that would end the Omega Experiment before it reached its goal. So, the gods held a meeting on the subject of the human future. The main issue was whether the gods could afford to leave humans alive, since the continuation of the experiment was paramount. If the humans were left unchecked, the whole experiment could go down the drain; if the gods picked another candidate species and started over, the experiment could continue, for Earth contained other species with basic social structures, like gorillas, ants, and bees. Some of the white-robed gods now leaned toward eliminating the humans, as they did with the dinosaurs, to maintain the experiment.

However, at the behest of the gods who had personally visited the Earth in various disguises and who felt most responsible and connected to the human destiny, humans gained a reprieve of fifty Earth years. If the humans didn't show enough advances in their collective consciousness, then it was agreed the gods would eliminate them. If enough positive changes were evident in human consciousness, then another meeting would be held to discuss possible further actions, if any. The gods put a number on the consciousness levels; ranking divinity as level 1,000, humans had to pass the consciousness level of 200, the point at which negative information could be converted into positive.

To act as a warning to the humans, the gods released a form of a virus that would be spread from one human to another through intimate physical contact, but one that humans would be helpless against. If humans had not made enough progress within these fifty years, then an airborne virus would be released and human extinction would begin. The gods also took care to warn several humans with higher-than-average spiritual sensitivity of the possible things to come and which signs to look for, telling them to warn their fellow human beings.

The white-robed gods took it upon themselves to help the humans avoid destruction by coming down to Earth again and spreading the message of spiritual enlightenment. Their efforts saw most effective and visible results in the last ten years of the fifty-year stay, with voices calling for spirituality and enlightenment getting louder with each passing year. At the end of the fifty years, the collective human consciousness had advanced far enough beyond the 200 level to escape from deliberate extinction.

The gods now embarked on a sudden-death game, thirty Earth years long. If humans, within those thirty years, either fall below 180 or go beyond 300, the game will end at that point. At 180 or below, the virus would be released immediately without further appeals or stays; at 300 or above, any plans to destroy the human species would no longer be pursued. After these thirty years, if the collective human consciousness level hadn't reached 300, the human experiment would be deemed a failure and be eliminated, ending the human period of dominance on Earth at a paltry 50,000 years.

The white-robed gods, pleasantly surprised at this hopeful turn of events, now pursued a more ambitious action plan to assist humans in their quest to reach the 300 plateau. The black-robed gods, complacent up until this point, now joined the act on the opposite side, for the result of this game would decide the operational direction of the universe, as agreed before.

The basic rule remained the same: although gods could walk and work among the humans, they could not use any of their godlike accouterments, giving only information to humans and leaving the final choice up to them. This sudden-death game is still going on today, with the collective human consciousness being measured every so often like a pulse. This game could end at any second, and even the gods hold their breath as to the outcome.

Which Side Are You On?

This scenario is not yet finished. It is in the middle of being written even now. We are all writing this scenario, shooting its scenes, editing the film. We are its originators, actors, and audience. How do you think this story will end? How do you *want* this scenario to end? Everyone has a role to play. Although your opinions may change, you can never escape from the role given you in this sudden-death game. Whether you realize it or not, you belong to one side or another. The fact that you might not be aware which side you are on cannot be an excuse for inaction, for you have intelligence and divinity. More importantly, you have a choice.

Your choice is that you can change your role. You can change sides. You won't be able to say, "I didn't know I was supposed to be a good guy. I was just following the lines." No, you write your own lines as you go on in this script. "I didn't know" will not be an excuse in this game.

If you would like to know on which side you belong in this grand game for human survival, examine your thoughts, words, and actions. Then decide whether your current role is to your liking. If not, change your team. There is only one choice, ultimately. Will you heal or kill? For myself, I choose to heal, for that was the result of perceiving my divinity within.

10th ENLIGHTENMENT

Ki, The New Universal Language

When someone asks, "Who are you?" we most often tell them our name. When someone points to an object and asks, "What is that?" we tell the person the name of the object. However, the name of the object is not the object itself. How far or deeply or truthfully can your name represent who you really are?

Since a name by itself is a poor substitute for a person, we use other names or titles to specify our existence in this society. I am so-and-so, the wife of so-and-so . . . I am a student at a such-and-such college majoring in such-and-such subject . . . I graduated from such-and-such school and am working for such-and-such corporation . . . . This goes on. However long a list you put next to your name, you will never be able to adequately express who you are. No matter how long a name may be, it is just a trademark or a label on you, but not you yourself.

What's in a Name?

A person's name, of course, is not the only kind of name in our language. Our linguistic system is composed of names. Nouns are names by definition; verbs are names of actions; and adjectives or adverbs are names of a shape or situation. Our awareness was trained and matured in this realm of names. Therefore, when we see an object, we automatically recall the name of the object, first and foremost.

Let's do a little experiment: what is in front of you? Whatever it is, can you see that object without recalling its name? It won't be easy. Whatever we see, we always call forth its name first. In the human consciousness, anything that has a form has a name. Perhaps we cannot see something unless it has a name. When you think you are seeing an object, therefore, what you are doing is reading its name. We see and understand objects through this window of the name. In other words, we live trapped inside a cage of information called the name, but we are so accustomed to it we don't see the bars.

This is similar to the way our brains function. In neurological terms, knowledge is a particular pattern of connections between neurons in the brain, and learning is a change or addition to that pattern of connections. For example, new knowledge will create a new neuronal connection. Strong preconceptions and ideas are represented by a long-lasting and strong pattern of neuronal connections, a hard-wired connection, so to speak. Memory is information contained within the neuronal matrix, which, when stimulated by energy, gets released into conscious awareness. A loss of memory implies that the connections that had formed the particular pattern representing specific knowledge are broken or dissolved.

This is the intimate relationship between hardware and software that even the most sophisticated computers do not have; it only exists in the brain. Therefore, it's not enough for you to *will* yourself to be free from the prison of names, for your brain (more specifically, the neocortex) is wired with this "name system." We could represent the informational prison as an inflexible matrix of neuronal connections.

Languages reflect the social values and beliefs of the society in which they are used. Therefore, when we name something, we are unconsciously and insidiously applying a value judgment about it already contained within the name. The value of an object in a society is also dependent on what uses it has to promote profit and livelihood in a market system. When we see a piece of wood, what name do you give it? Wood, timber, firewood, two-by-fours? All these names imply different uses for that same piece of wood. Your choice of a name betrays your intent, and it also reflects the system of value judgments of your society.

Ultimately, how close our social value system comes to reflect the life value system of the underlying truth of existence is dependent upon how closely language reflects the same, for our language and the associated value system are "hardwired" into our brains, as explained before. If the language we use is off the mark, we have no choice but to be off the mark also, for using such mis-guided language will force us farther from an understanding of the truth by the acts of speaking, writing, and communicating. We will look at the world upside-down. We will consider that we are suc-ceeding when in actuality we are failing; we will consider ourselves to be maturing when we are becoming more parasitic and depend-ent.

Some Things Cannot Be Expressed in Words

Although language has these inherent limitations, it has no problem when dealing with things in everyday life, such as drawing up contracts or writing a user's manual for machinery. It will con-tinue to be sufficient for such uses in the foreseeable future. We only come up against the limitations of language when we seek to express something that is beyond the realm of skills and/or tech-nology.

Have you ever felt frustrated because you could not put into words that deepest something within your heart? Say you had an insight of the truth, and you wanted to share that precious gift with as many people as possible. How would you explain this truth of complete and perfect life, of self-sustaining and eternal life? Because it is so difficult, some, like the Buddha, expressed it with silence, a flower, and a smile. But once that's done, people start to analyze and interpret the gestures and expressions; the smile means something, while the flower symbolizes something else, and so on.

These interpretations become recorded in a book and that book eventually becomes the sacred text of the tradition. Once it attains the level of a sacred text, the interpreted words gain and exercise an authority that controls and limits the behavior of people. People start to memorize, chant, and imitate the words of the sacred book. When the superficial gestures become ritualized and popularized, they get transformed into a religion, the essence of the insight long forgotten. Religions are products of interpretations that are, by definition, flawed.

Truth is truth, not the explanations of truth. Truth is a living, moving process. Truth is constantly undulating and vibrating. You can become one with the truth, but you cannot explain or even consciously recognize it. In order to recognize the truth, you have to separate yourself from it, and to explain the truth, you have to separate yourself from the recognition. This is an exercise of impossible prerequisites. This is why a wordsmithed truth is nothing but a shadow of the barest silhouette of the truth. If Buddha had yawned instead of holding up a flower, would that gesture have been any less representative of the truth?

It is sometimes possible to represent the truth with words. However, in that case, it is not the words themselves but the power of the vibration of the words as spoken by the speaker and the surrounding atmosphere that work together to make the speech into an experience, an entertainment event featuring the truth that allows you a tiny glimpse into the truth. But there is a world of difference in *being* at the "event" and *reading* about it in a newspaper article later on. Even if you had been there and felt the power of the event, you will be disappointed by the sterile words if you read the transcript of the same speech later on.

If you try to approach the truth only through words, this is akin to reading the transcript of the talk. Such is the limitation of language. Although it will do for our everyday lives, it is too small a vessel to hold the water of the truth and too rough a mesh to catch the flow of the truth.

Into the Sea You Go

We are not here to discuss the limitations of languages, however. Besides the truth, there are everyday experiences that often will not lend themselves to language. When we come across new experiences, we want to quantify and understand the experience; however, understanding an experience is the same as organizing the experience into words. When you say things like, "I don't understand what I went through . . ." or "I just have no idea . . ." you actually mean that you cannot find the words to describe your experiences. As our society becomes increasingly complicated and intricate, our experiences become more diverse, making it more difficult to put some realities into words.

Therefore, in an effort to quantify and put into language these experiences that we are constantly creating, we are inventing more words and terms and advancing the technology of informational processing to dizzying heights. Today, we have managed to quantify any and every word into binary bits, expressed in zeroes and ones. In this fashion, words become digitized signals and control machinery and computers.

Not only words, but light and sound can be transmitted in bits. CD players and digital cameras are prime examples of such technology. These advances, so often called the "Digital Revolution," are designed to make language more elaborate and sophisticated so that it can express our experiences more accurately. This process is akin to crowding tiny dots ever closer together so that they resemble a steady and consistent line.

Unfortunately, this is a game that we are destined to lose. We could apply all the latest technology and skills in the world but we still wouldn't be able to completely connect the space between two dots. Imagine two dots. Imagine the space in between. Draw a line that connects the two by crowding a straight path between the dots with tiny dots that will coalesce to look like a line. Then magnify the image. Are they completely connected or is there an empty space between the dot and the line and within the line itself?

Look at this empty space—there is infinity in there. Even the tiniest separation, too small even for a microscope to identify, contains infinite space. No matter how small the numbers—consider .00000000001 and .00000000002—there is an infinite space in between that you cannot fill even if all the supercomputers in the world tried for a hundred human lifetimes.

Take a digital camera and take a picture of the most beautiful flower you have ever seen. Now download this image into your computer and magnify it. Soon you will no longer see a flower or anything you can recognize. All you will see are dots of varying colors and spaces in between those dots. Then you will no longer even see the colors of the dots. They will just be jagged-edged blobs.

What happened to the flower, its petals quivering, sunlight glinting off the dew on its petals? The vibration of life you felt with this flower has disappeared into the digitized image. In like manner, truth and life cannot be captured by languages in any form—either in words or dots.

It is like trying to capture the sea by throwing a net into it. How can we catch the sea? Why do we keep casting the net? We should throw away the net and just jump into the sea, play with the waves and foam. The sea will receive you only when you throw yourself into it. You and the sea will become one. Only then can you say that you have "obtained" the sea.

Proof of Enlightenment

The only way that you can know the truth is to become the truth. The only way you can know life is to experience it through your body and become one with its flow. How? Ki is one way. Until now, Ki training was known as the secret to immortality in the Orient, considered to be incredibly beneficial to health. However, working with Zen *koans* (those puzzling questions) was considered necessary and essential to reaching a deep meditative state. The effect of *koans* and other meditative tools is to deactivate the logical circuit in your brain, thereby helping you sink easier into a world of no-language and affording you a glimpse into the eternal process of life.

However, what good is it if you could reach such an experience? What can you do with it, however profound, deep, and enlightening it is? What benefits can such an individual and isolated experience bring to the world? Since such experiences are by definition beyond language, they cannot be transferred to anyone else through language. But what else is there except for using language as a means of communication?

If an experience cannot be communicated so as to concretely change the society in which the experiencer belongs, then the experience has no power, even if the experiencer might be loath to admit it. We call a good experience that has no reality-based effect a dream. You just had a good dream. You can put a name to this dream. You can even name it "enlightenment," but nothing will have changed. Generally, people who have such an experience become attached to maintaining the feeling of this experience and grasp at its fleeting remnants. Although it is their choice whether to live in this dream world or not, the most truthful life I know of is to come back to everyday life and live it diligently to your utmost ability.

Therefore, I seek to talk about Ki, not immortality or dreamlike experiences. In earlier years, I sought to know the true essence of my existence and found, after a long and arduous process, that it was cosmic energy and cosmic mind. This is the essence of my "knowing." I realized that the life energy that animates my body is the same energy that flows through the cosmos. I realized that our minds and consciousness are connected to everything else in the cosmos through this flow of energy.

However I was not satisfied with this state of knowing. I wanted proof that my knowing had been true. I decided that my knowing had to be true if it could be shared with others. If a truth can be shared, communicated, and realized, then it is the truth. If not, I had just a beautiful dream, no more and no less.

Since then, I have spent all my time and efforts sharing my experience and realizing it in the real world. Of course, the act of sharing itself will not compel others to experience the same awakening that I have. That is an individual choice and cannot be made by anyone else. Knowing the truth of who you are and realizing it in real life are two separate things.

However, if everyone on Earth chose to be awakened to the truth of who they are, even if such awakening might not be immediately reflected in social actions, wouldn't this make our world so much better? We would come a lot closer to a healthy human society. This is the reason I teach Ki energy. What you do with it is up to you, but I can guarantee that by using it, as a minimum, your physical health will improve markedly.

What Is Ki, Anyway?

Ki exists everywhere. Ki is light, sound, and vibration. Ki does not exist solely inside a conceptual fence defined by terms such as yin, yang, or the Five Elements, as in traditional Chinese medicine. Ki exists beyond theories and beyond philosophy. Ki is the life that enjoys absolute freedom and cannot be confined by anything; it is the flow of life itself. Ki is the sea that cannot be caught by a net. Ki may become an object, phenomenon, or life. Coming together and drifting apart in an endless flow, Ki is the medium of expression of all phenomena of life. Not only the objects that surround us, but you and I are all temporary phenomena expressed by a coming together of the Ki flow that will soon dissipate and be on its way again.

Although we live immersed in this grand flow of Ki, as long as our sensitivity is not awake, we are not aware of the flow and do not sense the vibration of everything around us. Only when energy forms a solid object, thereby entering into the realm of the five senses, can we recognize it. Then we start naming everything, left and right, eventually imprisoning ourselves in names of our own making.

Strictly speaking, these seemingly solid objects are but temporary phenomena of a tightly packed energy flow, which makes all physical and tangible experience a Ki energy experience. Therefore, awakening your Ki senses is like expanding the tuning range on a radio to hear stations not normally heard, to include a range not covered by the five senses. Everybody is sensitive to Ki energy; how much and with what quality depends on the width of the "tuning range" and the sensitivity of your "antennae."

Our physical bodies contain several internal networks. Two are well known: the circulatory and nervous systems. The circulatory system carries nutrition and oxygen, while the nervous system carries information. The circulatory is a kind of plumbing system while the nervous system is like a telephone network. However, just because two bodies of water are connected by a pipe doesn't mean water will flow between them. For the water to start flowing, some type of a push, a motivating force, is needed. In the same manner, just because your telephone is connected through a switchboard to other telephones does not mean that you can talk with your neighbors without some type of power. The power that forces blood through the veins and arteries and information along the neural pathways is called Ki. The flow of Ki is the most basic flow of anything in the body.

But Ki also surrounds the body. To differentiate it from the physical and the spiritual body, we will call the cloud of Ki energy around the human body the energy body. Without the medium of energy, information cannot be realized in material form, just as you cannot access the information in a disk just by inserting it into a disk drive. You need an energy flow that delivers the information to the hardware to be expressed in whatever forms you want; only when electric current is passed through the disk will the information embedded be read and converted into an accessible form. Likewise, Ki is the medium by which information is carried *and* the net with which to gather it.

The routes through which Ki travels within and around our bodies are called the meridians. This is the third network, besides the circulatory and the nervous. However, meridians are not a set of physically constrained pathways to which the movement of energy is confined, but are specifically defined roads along the body through which the main flux of the energy travels.

Not only does energy flow in the meridians, but so does information. The information that is passed along the nervous system and the information passed along the meridians are different in nature. Quantitative information such as the pulse, blood pressure, and body temperature is passed along the nervous system, while more qualitative information, like feelings or moods, is delivered in the meridians on a wave of energy.

The nervous system can be said to take care of formal communication matters while the meridian system is in charge of informal communication. If you have ever done business or gone out on a date, you know that the informal communication of moods and feelings can be far more important than the formal spoken parts. If we were limited to only the formal mode of communication, we would never even have to see each other face to face. Everything could be done over the phone or by e-mail.

In such fashion, informal communication, the circulation and exchange of energy, maintains our life. Ki, therefore, fills many roles: it is the motivating force behind physical life functions such as the flow of blood or nerve signals, and it provides the communication channels that deliver information concerning moods and feelings. Ki is the analog information capable of filling in the "unfillable holes" left by digitized information. Ki is the language of life, the language of feelings, and the language of the soul. When you are feeling sad, the energy flow may be physically manifested as tears. When you are happy, the energy flow may be expressed as a bright expression and a light step. When these types of information are carried to the neocortex of the brain, we tend to make them wear different names, and call them "poems," "philosophy," or even "ideologies."

The Universal Language of the New Civilization

How can ants and bats know beforehand that an earthquake is coming? How can a salmon find its way back home? How can migrating birds orient themselves in the wide blue yonder? The amazing abilities of animals have been much talked about, but the exact mechanisms of these feats remain a mystery.

THE TWELVE ENLIGHTENMENTS FOR HEALING SOCIETY

Scientists suspect that animals are able to utilize their senses to detect changes to Earth's magnetic field. In fact, all life forms have the ability to detect minute changes in this energy flow. It's just that we humans have been dependent too long on recognition based solely on languages and thoughts and have not developed a finely-tuned sense for the energy. Therefore, in order to use the language of Ki, we first need to reawaken our inherent sense of the energy. This is not learning something new. This is not dangerous. And, it does not require tools or heavy lifting.

Since you already possess this sense, all you have to do is unblock the blocked parts and awaken the sleeping parts. Using the language of Ki does not go contrary to the use of language; actually, "Ki language" supports and enriches our word language, allowing us to experience those aspects of life that otherwise would have been impossible for us to contact. Remember the digitized dots? Ki language allows us to completely connect the space between the dots.

Although every experience that occurs in the world of the five senses is, strictly speaking, a Ki energy experience, you can directly experience Ki energy through three feelings: a sense of tickling electricity; a sense of pulling and pushing of a magnetic force; and a sense of alternating heat and cold. When your senses become trained through use, you can sense Ki as it moves through your mind. This, we call the language of the soul. Only then can you communicate and share with all of existence and fully utilize the information contained within the flow of Ki.

A sharing of the soul can only occur via communication through Ki. When this happens, you don't need scientific studies to tell you that the climate is warming, that species are disappearing by the hundreds every day, and that the rain forests are being destroyed. You don't need specifics; you can sense the deleterious effects directly. Just feel. Feel how the Earth feels. Feel how the sea feels. How the Heavens feel. How the universe feels.

Ki is the universal language we have to adopt to engage in spiritual growth. Ki is the universal language with the potential to help us overcome the national, religious, and ethnic boundaries that divide us today. Ki is the language of the soul that provides the path that will lead you to God, the cosmos, and ultimately, yourself.

Three Paths to Mastership: Principle, Practice, and Living

One of the most common questions I get asked during a lecture is this: "How can I become enlightened? How can I become a master?"

In the general parlance, a master is someone who has attained mental and spiritual mastery of herself. My questioners seem to be envious because they think I have attained something they want and they don't know how to get it. The unfortunate thing is that I have nothing to tell them, for there is no special way or method for enlightenment. Therefore, walking a path to enlightenment is an illusory exercise whereby you artificially build a path and try your best to stay on it. It's not that there is no path to enlightenment, but, more accurately, there is no distance between yourself and enlightenment across which you can build a road.

Enlightenment is our natural state of being. Since it is already us, you will never find it looking for it somewhere else. Why don't we know this? Why don't we feel this? Shouldn't we be able to recognize it if it is so close to us? Therein lies the contradiction. We cannot see it precisely because it is so close to us. Something that is too close or too large cannot be consciously recognized. Fish do not feel the reality of water since they live in it; we do not feel the flow of Ki although we live in it every waking moment.

The Difference between Enlightenment and Mastery

Let's think about a radar. The reason something like an airplane shows up on the radar screen is because it reflects back a signal beamed at it by the radar. Once that happens, the object becomes a bright dot on the radar screen. If there were no objects out there to reflect back the radar signal, then the radar would not register anything and the screen would be blank. There would be no recognition.

Usually, when we think we know something, this something corresponds to the bright dot on the radar screen because something has been spotted by the mental radar through the process of it being hit by a signal and hitting back. Knowledge is thus an exercise in collision. Your recognition and knowledge are like bright spots on the radar screen of your awareness.

Let's pause and ask, "What is knowing?" Are the bright spots on the screen "knowing"? Or is the constantly vigilant radar "knowing"? Knowing always happens whether you recognize it or not. However, when nothing is detected by the radar, there is no recognition of "me," for there is no reference point with which to define "me"; you have no thought about enlightenment nor do you think even for a moment that you have or have not attained enlightenment. The issue is moot without a sense of "me." Only when a bright dot can be recognized as "me" do you have these questions.

When a bright dot pops up on the screen, you concentrate on it, gradually realizing the separateness and incompleteness of the dot. So you try to collect as many dots on the screen as possible to fill the separateness, thinking that the preponderance of bright dots will eventually lead to the whole picture. However, enlightenment is the screen, not any dots on it, no matter how numerous. So you are trying to see the wholeness of the screen by covering it with more and more bright dots. How ironic. In fact, you cannot *not* know the "knowing" even if you tried, nor can you get rid of it, much like a wisp of cloud cannot exist without the sky, nor can it eliminate the sky.

I hope that you accept this basic logic of enlightenment and waste no more time in illusory pursuits, for you are only trying to gain what has already been given to you and is in your possession right now. Please do not use the "lack of enlightenment" as an excuse to put off your choices about life. The excuse that you are not enlightened is patently untrue, and enlightenment has nothing to do with the choice about how you should live.

Then what is a master? A master is someone who actualizes her enlightenment in everyday living. Everyone already knows what is right or wrong. But we do not admit that we know from right or wrong because we don't want to take the responsibility that comes with such an admission. We want to be able to plead ignorance when we do something that we actually know is wrong. A master is honest because he is someone who has chosen a conscious accept- ance of knowledge, knowing that responsibility comes with it. Knowing is not the same as acting. The choice to know and the choice to act on that knowledge are separate matters. A master is someone who has chosen not only to know but also to act, taking responsibility for his choices; such a life can be said to be beauti- ful and full of divine fragrance. A master consciously accepts his state of absolute knowledge, makes his judgment on the basis of this knowledge, and always chooses what he has deemed is right, taking full responsibility for his choices.

Most of us, because of our fear of responsibility, refuse to accept this state of knowledge. Even in acknowledging knowledge, we refuse to base our judgments on it. Even when we base our judgments on it and arrive at what's right, we refuse to make a cor- responding choice if it is not convenient. Even if we make the right choice, we refuse to take responsibility for it.

This is the difference between a master and a non-master. Fear and the consequent avoidance of responsibility are silly because we know (from previous chapters) that the universe is based on a system of absolute responsibility such that once you make a choice, the universe makes sure you take responsibility for it, even if this takes several lifetimes.

Dahnhak Is not a Technique to Attain Enlightenment

Dahnhak, which I have taught to millions of people for the last twenty years, is not a set of techniques through which you can attain enlightenment. If is it enlightenment that you wish, then there is nothing that I can do for you, for *Dahnhak* is not a way to gain enlightenment but a way to actualize enlightenment. *Dahnhak* is a way to train yourself so that you can actualize the choice you have already made based upon your enlightenment.

I have a goal for the life that I have chosen. Since it is my choice, I mean to take responsibility for my choice. The goal for my chosen life is to heal society and heal the Earth. *Dahnhak* is a set of principles and a system of methods with which I can achieve these goals. When you acknowledge your own enlightenment and seek to achieve the goal that you have chosen for yourself on the basis of your acknowledgment, then *Dahnhak* will provide you with useful information and tools. But if you still seek to attain a personal enlightenment, one that does not exist by definition, then *Dahnhak* has nothing to give you.

The underlying principles of *Dahnhak* have roots in an ancient philosophy and discipline of *ShinSunDo* (Way of the Divine Person, directly and inadequately translated), which was the founding principle and ruling ideology of an ancient Korean kingdom established more than 5,000 years ago. It was only recently that the tradition of *ShinSunDo* was revived and reworked into a modernized system of mind-body training.

There is no god to worship in this philosophy, no chosen people, and no set of rituals to follow to attain a god's love. The nucleus of this philosophy can be summarized thus: one, everything came from One and will go back to One; two, the One that exists within a human contains the Oneness of Heaven, Earth, and Human; three, life should be lived for the benefit of all life, not only for the family or tribe or group that you belong to.

The reason I have modernized this philosophy and teach it to as many as possible is that it corresponds perfectly to the truth I was awakened to, and because the philosophy is broad enough to include the whole of Earth on Her march to a worldwide spiritual civilization.

The essence of the *Dahnhak* educational system is not "studying" in the ordinary sense of the word, but it can be characterized more as the recovery of senses. The goal of *Dahnhak* is the recovery of the *Yuln'yo*, the natural rhythm of life that resides in humans and within all life, leading to a harmonious life. *Yuln'yo* is eternal life, light, sound, and vibration that exist wholly within and with itself. I describe this also as cosmic energy and cosmic mind. Even now, *Yuln'yo* is active within all life, beating and pulsing as the reality behind it. This is the energy that makes the Sun burn, Earth turn, and our hearts beat.

Dahnhak is an experiential educational system that helps people to recover the *Yuln'yo* within so that they would establish a harmonious relationship with each other, with nature, and ultimately become one with the grand harmony among Heaven, Earth, and Human.

A person who has recovered *Yuln'yo* in his heart I call "New Human" or an "Earth Human." A New Human has a capacity for love large enough to care not only for himself but for all existence. A New Human has a noble purpose that benefits the whole world. A New Human has commitment to and honesty about his purpose and can actualize it through living. A perfect human, an ideal human—it sounds glamorous, but it can be simple to achieve, for all you are doing is becoming what you were meant to be in the first place. You are becoming a healthy, beneficial human being.

Perhaps a New Human could also be termed "An originally intended human."

Five Qualifications for Being a New Human

First, you have to be healthy in body and mind. It may be too obvious to mention, but how can you help others and the world when you are not healthy yourself and need others' care instead?

It is in this vein that health is the most basic precondition to becoming a New Human. When I started the New Human movement twenty years ago, I started teaching calisthenics in a local park. However, more important than having a physically strong body is the establishment of a correct relationship between mind and body. Know who is the master. Be certain that health is needed not just to cater to the whims of the body.

Second, you have to be societally capable. You have to be able to take care of your own basic living needs, for how do you expect to help anyone else if you don't know where your next meal is coming from? This is why education is important, for it gives you the skills with which you can become self-sufficient in society. Societal capability can be defined as a combination of information and skills. There is no standard of information retention or skills achievement for you to be designated as a societally capable person, however, you should know and do enough to achieve the goals that you have chosen for yourself. For a person with a strong sense of life's purpose, diligence in learning knowledge and/or skills will be a given, for he knows he needs these to achieve his goals.

Third, you have to have a rich and spacious emotional life. Often we make the mistake of enviously thinking that someone who is devoid of emotions is someone free from them. However, there is a difference between non-sensibility and insensibility. A New Human exhibits the range of emotions: he gets angry when anger is justifiable, exhibits sadness when sadness is called for, expresses joy when joy is due. Emotion is not something to be suppressed and controlled, but something that must be enjoyed as a tool of life. Only when emotions are given natural and healthy rein will you be able to play well with others and with Nature, Earth, and Heaven. Therefore, a New Human is someone who plays well.

Fourth, you have to listen to your conscience. Just because it is obvious does not mean all people heed it. Conscience arises out of your love for the truth and desire to become truthful. Conscience is an expression of our perfectness, our divinity within. Because of the conscience, we instinctively seek to return to a state of perfectness if we step out of it, and to return to a state of balance when we have lost it. Without a conscience, health in body and mind, high intellect, and societal capability are tools that have lost their purpose. Even worse, without a conscience, these tools can be used to kill rather than heal as was intended. Conscience is an inner need for the truth and perfection based on our acknowledgment of the divinity within.

Fifth, you have to become divine. Divinity in life does not refer to a type of superhuman ability to see and hear things that normal humans can't. A spirit is information. Spirit is communicated through energy vibrations. When our brain waves are allowed access to the energy vibrations of the spirit, we are said to be inspired. Since all things in the universe are filled with spiritual energy, every existence is already divine. The level of divinity of a person, therefore, depends on the level of spiritual information. To be divine means you are privy to a higher quality of information.

Although the brain is open to all sorts of information, spirits, messages, and ideas, we have the option to choose which ones to accept or reject depending upon our taste and habits. At the basic level, it is a matter of the strength of your desire. In a bookstore full of many types of books, which one you choose is directly dependent on the strength and level of your desire for a certain subject. A divine person is thus someone who has a strong desire to benefit all of humankind, gathering and generating information productive towards that end. That's the kind of "book" such a person would choose.

All of the above is easier said than done. Although each of the five conditions is important individually, the most important part is strong desire and will to benefit the world, a desire that becomes lifelong. I call such a goal a vision. Only when used in accordance with such a vision can the New Human's tools and conditions fulfill their potential. By achieving your chosen goal through the use of these tools and conditions, you can realize and complete yourself. I call this the completion and perfection of the soul.

Soul is the seed of divinity within. The reason for our bodily manifestation on Earth is not to attain enlightenment (already given us), but to perfect the soul and help it blossom into a flower of divinity. Realization of enlightenment signifies the end of lost wandering and an entering of the correct path. This is why you will sometimes feel tired, frustrated, and even tempted to give up after enlightenment.

The journey is concluded only when the soul has been perfected by the completion of its original mission. Vision acts as the lighthouse that shows the path, so that we won't lose the way again. All the effort to actualize enlightenment in everyday living by reforming ingrained habits and nurturing good character goes to perfect the soul. This is the life of a New Human. This should be life of a *Dahnhak* practitioner.

Three Studies to Help Perfect the Soul

As long as your life's goal is the perfection of the soul, every moment and every situation is an opportunity for learning and growth. However, you may choose to consciously facilitate the process of the soul's perfection by pursuing these three studies: study of principle, study of practice, and study of living.

Study of principle signifies the realization of the truth; study of practice means internalizing the truth in your body; and study of living refers to actualizing the truth in everyday living. Through these studies, the soul will mature and eventually reach perfection. These studies are concrete and accurate and focus on the most important point. The preconditions most needed to successfully engage in these studies are not innate intelligence, money, or any special abilities, but honesty, diligence, and responsibility. No one can complete these studies for you.

The most fundamental of them is the study of principle. It is not a study that can be accomplished by reading books. The essence of this study is to realize the reality of the self, to know that you are the cosmic energy and the cosmic mind, to acknowledge perfect knowledge within. This is akin to knowing where the finish line is before starting a hundred-meter dash. To have a successful run, you have to know in which direction the finish line lies and to not lose that knowledge along the way. It is not a matter of running in general, but of running *toward* a specific goal.

Study of practice consists of making your actions consistent with what you know. By imprinting the acknowledgment of the truth into every bone and cell in your body, you are making your body and your actions an embodiment of the truth. Since truth's essence is zero, becoming an embodiment of the truth means that you are letting go of all the preconceptions, desires, and attachments you had been burdening yourself with. Information, in the guise of habits and memories, is lodged within us. Some information we are born with, some we pick up along the way, and some gets imposed upon us without our explicit permission. The study of practice means that we are reclaiming the original purity of life by eradicating all the information that litters us.

Third is the study of living, which means you actualize your enlightenment in your everyday life. Why do we need to do this? Why is meditating on mountaintops no longer sufficient? The reason we need this study is to judge and measure the progress of the soul. Soul is invisible to the eye, so, how can you tell how much the soul has grown? Through your character, for the latter is an accurate reflection of the maturity of your soul.

Character is formed through interactions with others during which we make choices, are judged by our choices, reflect upon others' judgments, and adjust ourselves accordingly. Although we suffer pain during this process, we may nurture a harmonious and virtuous character that resembles the Heavens and the Earth, a character unimpeded by obstacles. Since this can only be done in society where we coexist with others, the study of living is crucial.

Once a person thinks that he has realized the truth, there is a tendency to separate himself from the world. However, all you nurture in an isolated life is a sense of self-satisfaction and self-achievement without any actual growing of the soul. The soul grows by feeding on the joy, peace, and trust one gains by applying his enlightenment in the real world of everyday living. The soul, therefore, needs a mirror through which it can take shape and judge its own maturity. We need this, not for anyone else, but for ourselves, in order to help the soul mature and express its maturity through a good sense of personal character.

Rules for Masterful Living

Since the study of living must be done in the world, among people, an individual or an organization needs guidelines by which to plan and to apply the plan in the world. Without such guidelines, one is always nervous and unsure about the rightness of his decisions and actions, always waiting anxiously upon others' judgments or criticisms, being reactive to the situation instead of being proactive. Having guidelines that one can rely on and trust is akin to having a reliable compass when traveling along an unfamiliar road.

So how do you formulate guidelines? No need, for they already exists. We can divide the guidelines into three points, or rules. Rule One: Revolution vs. Rotation; Rule Two: Centripetal vs. Centrifugal Force; Rule Three: Fairness vs. Equality. These are the rules by which the universe runs. These rules are reflections of the cosmic mind. Some traditions call this the Tao, or the Way. These rules form the basic behavioral guidelines of all *Dahnhak* practitioners.

Rule One: Revolution vs. Rotation. The Earth spins on its own axis while revolving around the Sun. It creates a balance between a momentum towards a shared greater goal or central standard of value while effecting a personal and individual growth. As in all these rules, the order of the descriptive terms is crucial. Rotation must not come first, nor at the expense of the revolution, for you cannot put your own self-interest in front of the collective good. Should such a case occur, then the revolution itself will stop, resulting in an abrupt halt in the rotation. In a word, self-destruction would occur.

Rule Two: Centripetal vs. Centrifugal Force. When an object rotates around a central axis, the force that pulls the object toward the center and keeps it in a stable orbit and prevents it from flying off is called the centripetal force. The force always positioned at a 90-degree angle from the line of centripetal force, and that compels the object forward along the constantly changing direction of its momentum is called the centrifugal force (even though it is not technically a "force"). This is basic high school physics.

Imagine you are swinging above your head a sling whose pouch is filled with a rock. Your arm provides the centripetal force that keeps the rock from flying off into the air. The rock's tendency to fly off at every turn is provided by the centrifugal force. What would happen if the centrifugal force only acted on the rock? It would fly off, of course, to no constructive effect.

Only a combination of the centripetal and centrifugal forces keeps the rock in a proper orbit, balanced and full of potential constructive energy. Therefore, the centrifugal force (individual) must not become stronger than the centripetal force (community) for it would destroy the balance, the end result being that the individual flies off into oblivion.

Rule Three: Fairness vs. Equality. Fairness must come first, before equality, for the reverse situation breeds resentment and contempt, leading society into a morass of inaction. Case in point, the old Communist system. Since everyone was artificially positioned on an equal social and economic level, without regard to his or her respective contributions and talents, it was not a fair system. A fair judgment of the differences in ability, productivity, or situation must precede achieving balance in the community. Otherwise it is the same as giving the identical amount of food to a child and an adult and expecting them to do the same amount of work. Not only will this waste food, but it will create unrealistic expectations.

Therefore, equality must be preceded by fairness. In a society, fairness and equality represent a clear delineation of roles and responsibility for one's actions, followed by a fair judgment of the achievement or non-achievement of the individual. Only when this happens can we talk about honesty, diligence, and responsibility, the three mainstays of a healthy society.

If these rules are faithfully adhered to, then the community will function properly, no matter how small or large, from the nuclear family to the multinational conglomerate to the universe. If you don't maintain your proper "orbit" by working in sync with the center, you will collide with others; if you don't maintain a certain velocity to balance multidirectional forces, you will fly off into oblivion; and if you don't have a fair way to judge various inevitable differences in ability, productivity, and conditions, then you will not be able to maintain balance and harmony in a society.

Our social activities are maintained by adherence to these rules. Our bodies are a prime example of such a "society." Our cells are not automatons, to do as they are told. Each cell has a set of possibilities to choose from, for it contains all the information to become anything in the human body. However, the cells align their "choices" to the needs of the whole. Our body's organic order was not imposed by an external force, but is a self-organizing and self-maintaining system. It truly is a miracle. And it's only possible because each and every cell keeps to the three rules discussed above.

Societal Mastership

When we seek to apply these principles to society at large, the important thing is to accurately determine what is the center of all these movements. If all societal activities are aligned to the three rules as described, what is the ultimate center that can act as the final and comprehensive standard for all such activities? Where is the Sun around which our societal "planets" orbit in harmony? Where is the central axis around which our activities and actions revolve as they rotate? How can we apply these principles to all human activities? The answer is literally below our feet: Earth.

From Earth's point of view, the human species is not special above all the others, and certainly not any one specific people's culture, religion, and gods. If we place our own religion, gods, and people as the central standard of social values and activities, then we break the harmony, and that will lead to the destruction of order, peace, and finally, of ourselves. Placing Earth as the final arbiter of our activities is the way to save Earth and to achieve our salvation.

Without these rules, no one movement or event or civilization can go on for long, no matter how strong its momentum may be at the start. A cell that does not think first about the whole organism, a team member who does not follow the team's wishes—a nation or a religion that does not align itself to the needs of the whole Earth—these can be described as cancers. What does a cancer cell do? Destroy the organism and ultimately itself in an orgy of individual, isolated frenzy.

So what does mastership signify? How does a master act? A master sustains the natural order of the universe by following the three rules in all his actions, including speech. A master realizes that the three rules represent the operating axioms of the universe, that they are a reflection of the cosmic mind itself. Order and harmony will appear when these rules are adhered to, while chaos and conflict will rule when they are ignored. The flow of cosmic energy and cosmic mind, although invisible, continues uninterrupted and unimpeded, consistently and forever, never late nor early. This flow of the essence of the cosmos bathes us with its immeasurable love and guides us with its austere mercy, for only through the austerity of its mercy can all life gain an opportunity to realize itself in safety.

12th ENLIGHTENMENT

Our Assignment—Civilization Shift

The daydream we most often enjoyed when we were little was probably of the "What if I were older?" variety. This daydream is only possible when the future is wide open, providing an infinite variety of dreams, limited only by the range of our imagination. A wide-open future always gives us joy, for it gives our dreams and hopes a spacious canvas on which to paint. Having a future, by definition, means the possibility of a choice. To be able to choose—do any one of us truly know the deep significance and feel a keen appreciation of this? A future without the possibility of choice is a dead future, a closed future, a non-future. How fortunate we are that we can still choose.

However, the future is not always guaranteed to be always wide open. Our choices today may open up the future, but they can also close it. The reason we exist today is because our forefathers had the wisdom to make choices that left the door to the future open for us. The future is, therefore, not a right but a responsibility. We don't have the right to close down the future; we have only the responsibility to keep it open.

Choose Now for Ten Years Hence

Let us daydream awhile. When it's ten years from now, what will you be like? What kind of Earth will we have? Will we still have the luxury of dreaming about another ten years down the road? All this depends on how we use the most precious gift that the creator has given us: choice. The possibility of choice, however, also contains the right to give up our choice.

Going on the same path, even when we realize that it is a dead end, is an act of giving up our right to choose and closes down the possibility of future choices. Although we can take this road, we don't have the inherent right to do so. On the contrary, we have a responsibility to not continue on this dead-end path; the responsibility is not for our descendants but ourselves. Time flows quickly and our future draws ever nearer. To be able to still imagine ten years from now ten years from that, what can we do now? What do we have to do to leave the door open to the future possibilities beyond ten years from now? This is our "homework" as humanity. I call it a civilization shift. A civilization shift would be a first in the history of humankind, although we have heard legends of long-gone civilizations that disappeared because they failed to effect such a shift.

We are still running down the same road as our ancestors, not because we are absolutely sure that this is the right road to be on, but because we have an amorphous and unrealistic expectation that nothing too terrible could happen to us, or that someone somewhere will solve large problems that come our way. Only now are we feeling nervous. We are slowly realizing that the bus we are on does not have a driver. Our scenery from the bus windows is getting bleaker and the speed seems to be picking up. We are realizing that we might crash into a mountain or fall off a cliff at this rate. We realize it will be difficult to stop and change directions.

This is the reason for the increase of collective anxiety on Earth. A poet might write this feeling with a poem about Hell's gate opening up; priests might conjure images of apocalypse; and an engineer might use the term "non-sustainable, closed-end system." They would all be speaking about the same thing. How about you? Where do you think we are heading to? I am not a poet, priest, or an engineer, but my instinct tells me, my enlightenment that allows me to see one finger as one finger tells me, it's time for us to shift direction.

Outside In

Where should we start? What should we start with? If we were to attempt to change the social infrastructure in a day, the stress and strain of such an effort would probably destroy civilization itself. How can we turn this "bus" around without an abrupt stop that would throw everything into chaos? How much has to change for us to call it a fundamental change? Our conscious, and even our unconscious, thoughts have an innate desire to be realized. It is not our conscious desire to achieve something; rather it is a fundamental need and desire to be realized, to take some type of a form and shape, embedded within all life, that is the driving force behind all growth. Therefore, our desire for growth lies outside the realm of conscious choice, outside civilization, for it is a function of life itself.

A life created, whether it belongs to a civilization or not, has an instinctive drive to realize its potential and leave seeds behind. This does not mean that we are helpless to stop the bus; it just means that, although we may not be able to stop it, we are able to choose its direction so as to guarantee our further growth.

The direction in which our civilization has been headed until now was always to the outside of things. "Faster, higher, and stronger" is not just an Olympic motto, it is a self-declaration of civilization. Such a movement toward externals, the outside, is inevitably expressed through activities characterized by possession and domination. The results are always more land, more money, more power in an inevitable spiral of "better and more" that leads to competition and divides us into winners and losers.

Since sharing the pie would decrease the size of one's own

piece, monopoly and absolute control drive the day. On the other hand, a direction toward the inside of things, towards an inner civilization, leads us to strengthen our powers of love and peace, which are expressed through actions such as forgiveness, reconciliation, and calmness. Since this direction leads to perfect completion instead of victory, sharing does not decrease my lot. My soul's perfection does not prevent others from reaching their perfection, and my sense of peace does not lessen because I freely share it with others.

Human civilization until now expressed its instinctive desire to grow by worshipping the body and pursuing external powers. We have come to realize that this direction will not support us forever, it is not sustainable. This is not a value judgment of good versus evil on our current civilization, it is an objective and impartial observation. The reason we have to effect a shift in our civilization is not that our civilization is evil or weak, but that it is not sustainable in this form.

Paradigm Shift: Duality to Trinity

Despite the countless changes in external appearances, actors, and players, our civilization—this version anyway—has had a consistent philosophical base in duality. You and I, yin and yang, this and that, white and black, good and evil, god and devil, and so on. This duality is ingrained now, the glasses through which we understand and seek to understand everything in the universe. Competition and domination, the basic driving forces in our society, are offspring of duality.

What, then, is the alternative to duality? What can fill the gulf between God and Satan? What is the "middle" that we have forgotten and need to recover? The answer is life, energy (Ki), and the Human, especially a new understanding of the Human. The human, instigator and protagonist of creation, is the key to overcoming the inherent flaw of duality. I choose to call this grouping Trinity.

In a world of duality, humans are no better than a passive part, ingredients that make up the material world. Throughout history, humans were slaves to gods; humans were victims or destroyers of nature. In economics or social studies, humans are defined as a commodity that follow a set pattern according to the forces of the market economy. In biology or anatomy, humans are a complicated collection of cells and organs. In none of these learned fields is the idea of spirit given any consideration.

Spirituality is the perfect knowledge that we are all born with; it is enlightenment. We may call it divinity or conscience. Conscience is different from ethics or morality as taught in society, rather, it is an instinctive drive and will toward the truth. Conscience is an expression of our internal perfectness and divinity.

Spirituality is the bridge that connects us to the ultimate source of all existence, the sea of nothingness. Therefore, a spiritual awakening is reestablishing the connection to the source, discovering your own roots, in a sense. The first order of business that we must accomplish in order to know our roots is to know the root of our physical manifestation first and foremost: Earth, to know that your life and Earth's life are not separate but one, that you are a part of the great biosystem called Earth.

To arrive at such a realization, we have to overcome the psychological obstacles of nationhood, religion, and race. We have to realize that these barriers are artificial and temporary, more illusions than reality, and recover our sense of being of the Earth, for the Earth, and by the Earth. A person of Trinity is a person who has realized his own spirituality, acknowledged his inner enlightenment, and overcome all prejudicial senses of group identity. This is an Earth-Human.

The most fundamental living philosophy on Earth is the philosophy of *HongIk*, translated from the Korean as "Wide Benefits." It refers to the desire to spread benefits to the world, not because someone demands or forces it, but because such actions are essential to your self-identification as an Earth-Human. The concept of the Earth-Human is the nucleus of the civilization shift our world requires today. In an historical context, it signifies the rediscovery of what it means to be human, or it could be the first-ever discovery of what it means to be human, for no civilization before us has achieved such a momentous shift that we know of. It also signifies our willingness to take responsibility for the choices in regard to our future. Knowing well that our lives and future and the future of Earth depend on our choices, we choose to take on the burden.

This paradigm shift represents the philosophical prerequisite for the new politics and economics of the new civilization. What should we call this new civilization? I choose to call it the spiritual civilization, not to distinguish it from the material one we live in today but to emphasize our absolute knowledge in the limitations of a material civilization.

Material objects in this civilization will not be the end itself, but a means to grow a soul. This new civilization will not hate materials nor give up the notion of material advances. However, we will define growth and maturity in a new directional sense. Spiritual does not stand on the opposite shore from Material as far as civilizations go, but the former encloses and surpasses the latter.

Assignment: Civilization Shift

All these changes will begin when our goals and our ideas of growth change. From such a point, a basic series of changes to our way of living will follow, eventually resulting in a quiet but inexorable shift worthy of being called historic. It will be a shift from a non-sustainable to sustainable civilization, from material-worshipping to a material-utilizing civilization; from success-pursuing to a civilization desiring a perfection of the soul of its people.

It will also be a shift from a hypercritical civilization in which ideals and reality betray each other, to an honest and conscientious one in which your life is an accurate representation of the truth in your heart. It will be a shift from self-destruction to self-nurturance, from the powers of destruction to the powers of healing, from a world of Jews, Arabs, Americans, Chinese, to a world of Earth-Humans, of spirituality.

It will be a shift from a parasitic civilization that cannot safely dispose of its own garbage to a mature civilization that will pick up what it has dropped, replant where it has harvested, and rejuvenate when it has withdrawn substance. From a foolish civilization where history tends to repeat itself to a wise civilization that realizes that the Heaven, Earth, and Human Trinity is the basis of all existence, and which takes responsibility to actualize the bright light of enlightenment within. From a world where people live in isolation and non-communication in a sea of information to a world where all of the Earth will communicate freely. From a civilization lorded over by a small group of political or spiritual elitists who uses violence and coercion as common tools to a world where enlightenment is the same as common sense.

How will you accept such a civilization shift? For many people, this sounds like an impossible dream. However, this is not a matter of reinventing the wheel but of adjusting the steering; it depends on our choice. Let's start small. Let's start by waking up our dormant senses first. We don't lack for information. What we lack is not information but senses, senses that will digest the warnings and danger indications and imprint upon us the gravity and seriousness of the situation we face now. When we have awakened these senses, we can begin the transformation. Let us all awaken these senses that will allow us to communicate with one another and with the Earth in a way that no languages enable us to do.

Enlightenment is not far off. Actually, it can't be closer than it is now. Let's no longer put off our own heritage of enlightenment. Let's choose to acknowledge our own enlightenment—this is the first choice. This choice will bring us the clearsightedness to see the world as it really is, the honesty to judge what we have done so far, the diligence to actualize the choices we have made, the responsibility to accept the results of our choices. In the process of choosing and actualizing enlightenment, a new set of habits will be formed, a new personal character will emerge, and a new civilization will be built.

Education develops character in humans, so the educational system should be the first thing to change. Rather than focusing on the public school educational system, your in-home education must be changed. Parents must once again take on the role of enlightened educators who can communicate their Earth-Human awareness to their children. An Earth-Human parent is a teacher, healer, and an activist at home.

A teacher who helps children awaken their self-identity as Earth-Humans and choose life goals commensurate with such an identity, a healer who is skillful enough to care for his family's mental and spiritual health, and an activist who lives what he preaches at the ground level—this is what we need. When parents fulfill their roles as teachers, healers, and activists, the home will be the organic impetus that compels society to resurrect its fallen central pillar of value and recover its role as a community. Changes at home will expand to changes in other parts of society, plowing a strong and reliable field in which the seeds of Earth-wide change will sprout.

Another Sun to Brighten the Earth: SUN

An Earth-wide change is obviously beyond the realm of any individual or family unit. An Earth-wide change is likewise impossible for any one organization or country to effect, no matter how large or strong. It is only possible when a spiritual alliance of Earth-Humans is formed that supersedes any religious or national or ethnic affiliation. Although we don't yet have such an organization, if there were one, I would like to call it SUN.

SUN is the Spiritual Union of New Humans, an association of New Humans who have chosen to actualize their acknowledged enlightenment by healing society and Earth. SUN is the Spiritual Union of NGOs, an alliance of nongovernmental organizations that are going beyond political and territorial barriers to realize love for humanity and love for Earth. SUN is the Spiritual Union of Nations, an alliance of nations that acknowledges that we are all Earth-Humans despite our religions and ethnic differences. SUN is ultimately the Spiritual UN, an organization that will support the UN in its original goal of the eradication of the disease of war, and which will become active in the promotion of cultural and non-political activities designed to bring people together. SUN is all these and more. SUN is the Sun that will brighten and warm the new spiritual civilization.

SUN does not indicate the birth of another organization, for our civilization will not change just because a new organization is registered, board members appointed, and by-laws adopted. Humans have to change in a fundamental way, or nothing will happen. Our social values must change, our attitude toward life must change, and the basic nature of our desires and ambitions must change, from outer to inner, from external to internal, from winning to perfecting. Therefore, SUN, when it becomes a reality, will represent a new value system, a new character, and a new way of life for a New Human.

If only 1 percent of the Earth's population will choose to live in the future and choose to undergo a personal civilization shift, then Earth's destiny will change. Considering that most studies indicate that Earth's population will reach ten billion in the near future, 100 million New Humans, 100 million Earth-Humans, 100 million strong healers of society and the world, can pioneer a shift in civilization, combining their strength focusing their power of enlightened vision on the SUN to effect a true change and kick the door to the future wide open. This is the future I envision in ten years. Now is the time to make the choice. You have to make the choice, for no one else will. The start of a new civilization begins with you.

WALSCH

BOOKS

Visions of the Spirit

WALSCH BOOKS is an imprint of Hampton Roads Publishing Company, edited by Neale Donald Walsch and Nancy Fleming-Walsch. Our shared vision is to publish quality books that enhance and further the central messages of the Conversations with God series, in both fiction and non-fiction genres, and to provide another avenue through which the healing truths of the great wisdom traditions may be expressed in clear and accessible terms.

Hampton Roads Publishing Company

. . . for the evolving human spirit

Hampton Roads Publishing Company
publishes books on a variety of subjects including
metaphysics, health, complementary medicine,
visionary fiction, and other related topics.

For a copy of our latest catalog,
call toll-free, 800-766-8009,
or send your name and address to:

Hampton Roads Publishing Company, Inc.
1125 Stoney Ridge Road
Charlottesville, VA 22902
email: hrpc@hrpub.com
www.hrpub.com